SELF MASTERY
FOR SUCCESS

Unlock Your Ultimate Health & Prosperity Power From the Inside Out

by DR. STEPHANIE KABONGO, MD

Published by Innovation Publishing, Best Seller Success (USA)

First Trade Paperback Printing July 2013

Copyright © 2013 Stephanie Kobongo All Rights Reserved

ISBN: 978-1-922093-17-2

Moringa Better Life Ltd
No 6 Doreen Street,
Colbyn, Pretoria
0083, South Africa

Disclaimer

The information provided in this book is designed to provide helpful information on the subjects discussed. This book is not meant to be used, nor should it be used, to diagnose or treat any medical condition. For diagnosis or treatment of any medical problem, consult your own physician.

The publisher and author are not responsible for any specific medical or health needs that may require supervision by a licensed healthcare practitioner, and thus they are not liable for any consequences from any recommendation, to any person reading or following the information in this book.

Portrait Photographer: Linda Bell +855 12 774 214 (office@belatel.com), location Auckland New Zealand.

In Praise of Self Mastery For Success

Self Mastery For Success covers the broader definitions of health, considering its physical, mental, emotional, social and spiritual aspects, which are closely linked. Wellness involves a balance of the several dimensions of life, and your behaviors and beliefs determine your success in each of these areas. This is not an easy task, and it takes a great deal of self-knowledge. This book will help you focus on the things you can change, with several tips to improve your well-being.

What if we create all the difficulties in our life by our own choices, and whatever we are experiencing is the result of our past decisions? At some point, we need to learn to make better decisions, and reading this book, today, is an excellent start in that direction.

Sir Kenneth Miller, CIPS RRP AMS, Author: *Enter Crying, Exit Laughing©: Delay Dropping Dead and Live a Hot, Happy & Healthy Life* **CEO, Global Marketing Group Limited, New York, New York Executive Director, United Nations Centre for Human Settlements**

"Self Mastery For Success" spoke to me on many different levels. As a medical doctor who had a short stay in hospital after an operation, the author, Stephanie Kabongo, discovered that being a patient was far from being a positive experience and she vowed to make the necessary changes to ensure that her patients had a far better experience when under her care. She became aware of the need to treat the whole person; body mind and spirit and set about developing a health coaching practice based on those areas…

If you want to learn about how to have a completely holistic approach to your life and your health and wellbeing you will find everything you need in this book

Janet Matthews, Dip ION

Author of *Is Stress YOUR Silent Killer? How to deal with stress and achieve permanent stress relief and Really Healthy Gluten Free Living: Your diet may be gluten free but is it healthy enough to heal your gut?*

In this remarkable book Dr Stephanie Kabongo explains in simple to understand language that health and success in all areas of our life can be achieved if we are prepared to embrace the very real power of positive thinking. As a Medical Professional Dr Kabongo has combined her years of medical training with a holistic approach to help her patients achieve optimum health, success and prosperity.

Having been on a journey with a close relative battling depression I can fully attest to the power of positive affirmation. Self Mastery for Success is a must for anyone who is looking for the power to change their life.

Julia Beverley Mather, Social Media Copywriter

Dr Stephanie K has the skill of explaining the complex human mind, in a way that is easy to understand and convert into strategies we can use every day.

This book is a fresh and exciting view of the human mind and body. It deals with the issues that we ALL face... Stress, health, attitude... And gives actions to eliminate the negative from our lives so we can be the best version of ourselves.

It's easy to read, entertaining and crucial!

This book is the foundation for life knowledge and personal growth.

Jody Jelas, JodyJelas.com

It's refreshing to read a book written by a doctor that focuses on the power of thought and emotions, and offers easy simple steps you can take to improve your health and your life. More and more, fortunately, doctors are starting to treat their patients as whole beings, not just as their symptoms.

The author writes like she is talking to a friend, and offers examples that you can relate to. I caught myself smiling more than once recognizing a few of my self-sabotaging behaviors. And the good thing is that it's never too late to change for the better.

Getrude Matshe, Account Manager
Medical Recruiters of NZ Ltd

Contents

Dr. Stephanie Kabongo

Meet Dr. Stephanie Kabongo

Dr. Stephanie K is a medical doctor who also works as a health and a success coach. Her passion for helping people lose weight, get healthy, and achieve their success goals in life is well recognized because Stephanie understands the struggles of her clients, as she personally has had to overcome many huge obstacles in her own life.

She struggled to get through medical school in a tough, racially charged university. She then immigrated as an African woman to a new country, far away from her friends and family support, where life was less than ideal.

It took a great deal of mind setting to achieve success in a new country as an immigrant, but Stephanie did it. She's no stranger to hard work and overcoming challenges.

Today, Dr. Stephanie K uses her experience, her failures, and her triumphs to motivate her coaching clients and her seminar audiences to achieve more in their own lives.

Her Realization…

The pivotal point that set her on the right path occurred when she was forced to see life in a new light. She stepped out of her own reality, and saw the reality of those around her who were worse off than she was.

This realization is what Stephanie credits for the changes that have taken place in her career, her health, and have helped her build her own success as it is today.

This realization occurred whilst Stephanie was in a hospital bed after a routine operation from an old hip injury. Dr. Stephanie Kabongo had a life-changing insight; it was an 'Oprah moment' of sorts.

Stephanie, as a patient, describes her experience in that hospital as one of the lowest points in her life. She was so used to being the doctor, and now she was the patient lying in bed, waiting for the doctors to come in the ward rounds. It was a strange role reversal, which turned out to be a miraculous life-changing event for her.

It was a new hospital, and they had forgotten to put her title "Dr." before her name, so it was her secret. Thus, she was treated just like every other patient in the hospital.

During these ward rounds, Stephanie felt as if the ticking clock was more important for the doctors than she was as a patient. She also sensed this whole experience as being just strange, now that the tables were turned.

In hospitals, ward rounds usually are quick, to make sure each patient is seen to. As is the standard procedure, when the Doctors arrived at Stephanie's bedside, they pulled back the curtains and talked to each other about her post-operation status, then removed the bandage from her large surgical wound, looked at it and commented that it was healing well. What they didn't do was talk to her, only among themselves and before leaving.

It was shocking to see them just walk away, without taking the time to talk to her as a patient or as a human being, a person coping with the wound they were examining. Again, without conferring with the patient, the doctors ordered the nurse to take 'the wound patient' to rehab, and after that, get her discharged home in two days. That was that.

They talked *about* her, as if she wasn't even there in the bed in front of them.

Stephanie was shocked at their insensitivity. This was a really startling experience. Her mouth dried, and she couldn't speak because she was so aghast at how badly this must come across to all patients in general. She describes this as feeling totally worthless as a human being. Stephanie often talks about this saying:

> "As a hospital doctor myself, I had been doing ward rounds just like those doctors who saw me. In my moment in that hospital bed, I was shocked and disgusted at how it felt to be their patient. In that life-changing moment, I made my decision never to treat patients that way. I committed to always have a holistic approach to patient care, which takes their feelings and wellness into consideration."

This role reversal incident indeed reawakened the doctor/healer inside Stephanie as to what it feels like to be a patient under her own care.

In that moment, Dr. Stephanie realized she never wanted to make anybody feel as terrible as she did that day, and that she could give more, go deeper, and help people heal in ways that honored them as whole, loving and complete beings. She made a decision then to begin a journey that would change her life and the lives of her patients and clients.

> *Dr. Stephanie Kabongo is a leading authority on health and success breakthroughs. She will teach you how to achieve your success and a stress-free life... no matter your starting point.*

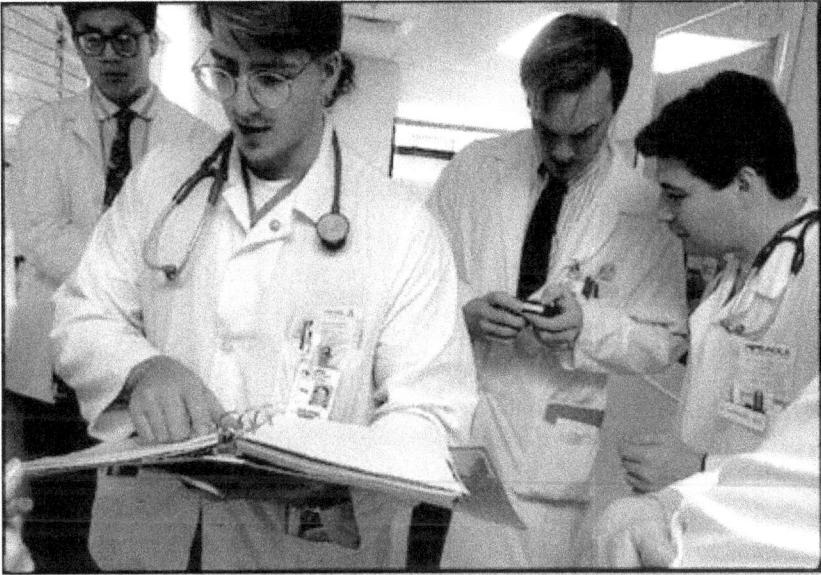

Moving forward...

After her trauma of being a hospital patient, who felt little better than a number on a form, Stephanie changed her focus to help others achieve their ultimate in personal success, health, and well-being through holistic success coaching and natural health.

Her journey as a well-respected MD included a special interest in health and wellness, related to stress management. Her study of the effects of stress on the human body and the mind has led her to further education in Public Health, nutritional medicine, natural hormones, anti-aging and regenerative medicine.

Stephanie uses natural alternatives wherever possible, including health coaching, Bio-Identical Hormones, organic herbs and supplements. She is passionate about people's success, health and happiness.

> *"I discovered that empowering people to succeed in life, improves their health and energy levels. It gives me the greatest satisfaction in my career and my life to witness that occurring."*

Dr. Stephanie's core mission is to help people eliminate struggle, failures, and un-healthiness from their lives and to have a successful and stress-free life! She works with clients on achieving success, losing weight, stress-related conditions, hormone imbalance, anxiety disorders, burnout, adrenal fatigue, etc. With her help, her clients are able to overcome their struggles, their stress, and burnout with simple and effective techniques. They regain their health, success, happiness, and vitality.

One of the ways she does this is through one-one coaching, group coaching, mastermind groups, and live in-person events where she inspires others to transform their lives.

As a trained medical doctor, she has a vast knowledge about the effects of stress on the human body, such as hormonal imbalance, mental disorders, and more. She uses her medical resources to the client's advantage and satisfaction, and helps them lose weight the natural and holistic way.

Dedication

This book is dedicated first to the deep gratitude I have for Almighty God, the Creator of all and to His son, my Lord and Savior Jesus Christ.

I am grateful for my ability to motivate, inspire and communicate these health and success coaching lessons I have discovered through my natural medicine career, and through consistent study of self-development teachings, books and seminars.

I also dedicate this book to my loving, caring and supportive family and friends, as well as to those who are struggling to succeed in health or in life goals.

My final dedication is to those who choose to persist, and refuse to accept failure or to settle for less than they deserve. This is for all the men and women who know that they deserve success, and who are willing to keep learning new ways to thrive in their lives, despite all odds. Success is coming, and it will meet you on your way! You are closer than you think! Keep the faith alive! Never give up!

Foreword

As busy entrepreneurs, mentors and speakers we are very blessed to travel the world often, meet and connect with large groups of wonderful people, and help others to achieve their dreams, success and marketing goals.

We love our work, even with the busy scheduling, and have to manage priorities in order to accomplish everything we do. So it has become imperative to live a very healthy life that energizes us to enjoy our travels and success.

When we started our company Launch You Now, two years ago, we had no way of knowing that we would be living the extraordinary and blessed life that we are living today. With hundreds of international graduates having successfully completed our training programs, we are so fortunate to still have robust health and what a blessing. With our lifestyle we need it! But it wasn't an accident that we have such good luck. It is the result of good health coaching, focus and mentoring.

We love our business and community and so keeping in top shape health-wise has become one of our most important priorities. We have learned to develop a very healthy way of living that gives us power, vitality and energy!

When a rare synergy occurs and we meet a wonderful woman with a mission to share her lifetime of experience as a medical practitioner, who teachers about the body, mind, and spirit and your connection to Source energy as this relates to your prosperity consciousness; we feel honoured to be able to introduce her vital work to others, and to present it to help eliminate many of the health issues so many are plagued with today, which are so often totally avoidable.

Dr Stephanie K took a career in medicine because she wanted to help people improve their health, lives and wellness. But after 14 years as a medical doctor seeing clients 15 minutes at a time she realized she must start spreading her lifetime of knowledge to much larger numbers of people world-wide in order to fulfil her destiny as a health, wellness and success mentor.

In this book Dr Stephanie demystifies complex topics and has applied them as they relate to greater success in life and in health. Her work in coaching, workshops and seminars has helped thousands of people to achieve provable results. She has transformed her own practice into a mission of spreading knowledge to groups of people in person or via Skype, fulfilling her life purpose as a healer and mentor world-wide.

Dr Stephanie's thousands of clients have taken her advice and proven health, happiness & success in their lives. That qualifies her as an expert in the health and success field who can help you achieve optimal health and transformation of your own life and wellness.

Her core mission in life is to help people eliminate struggle, failures and un-healthiness from their lives and to live a successful & stress-free life! With her help, her clients are able to overcome their struggles, their stress and burn out with simple and effective techniques. They regain their health, success, happiness and vitality.

One of the ways she is best known for doing this is via one on one coaching, group coaching, mastermind groups and live in-person events where she inspires others to transform their lives.

As a trained Medical doctor, she has a vast knowledge in the effects of stress on the human body such as hormonal balance, mental disorders etc... She uses her medical resources to the client's advantage and satisfaction.

It is our pleasure to introduce her book to you so that you may achieve better health, prosperity and results in life too.

Lynn Rose and Bob Doyle

International Speakers, Law of Attraction experts, and creators of the "Launch You Now" program, www.LaunchYouNow.com

Introduction

To my beautiful friends, I first want to thank you, and congratulate you for buying my book. It is not every day that you discover a book that teaches you how to appreciate yourself, your health and your success, regardless of your stage in life.

By reading this book and applying what you learn, you'll change the way that you view your body, the way you view your health, and your path to success in life will be simpler. Let me begin with the concept of:

Every aspect of you is interconnected...

You are the common denominator in your health, your success, your relationships, and in everything in your entire life. By reading this book, you will view yourself in a completely new way; one that you probably have not seen before. After reading this book, you will feel a different connection to your body, an improved connection to your success, and an enlightened connection to your environment.

The only thing I ask is that you have a relaxed approach as you read the book, extract what resonates with you, and apply it to your new way of doing and being.

This book doesn't discriminate against anyone or anything. It was written to unite all who are looking forward to succeeding with health and life goals. It was written so that anyone can enjoy making the changes in their daily life, supportive of improved health, well-being and success.

Improvements can begin in anyone's life, no matter whether they are the leader of the pack, or just beginning their journey. One key to remember is: it's not how you start that matters... but THAT you start – that is what's important.

We all have the ability to succeed in everything we set our minds to accomplish in our lives… without exception. Health is simply a success goal, just like any other, and all success goals are absolutely achievable.

Attaining great health is your innate birthright. It is not a "reserved only table" for the special ones. It is within reach of all of us. Even though many people fail at the success goals of money, good health, and weight loss, I believe that with more knowledge and the empowerment of principles, that can easily change.

Self Mastery

Self mastery empowers you with a winning mindset to tackle any success goal, including health and losing weight. It is not just limited to health; the principles also apply to career choices and all relationships in your life.

The Importance of Getting the Proper Mindset and Clarity

Without the right mindset, you will struggle forever with attempts at achieving anything and everything. One of the first things you have to accomplish is a winning mindset, your winning mindset.

If weight loss is your goal, then I suggest you apply the principles that are believable and applicable for you.

Some techniques that you'll learn with me will put you in a space of knowing what you really want to achieve in life. You will become clearer and more focused on your success goals. Once you have that clarity, and I truly believe that clarity is power (more on that later), you will achieve more of your goals because you are becoming absolutely clear as to exactly what those goals are.

Even your attitude and associations relating to your goals must change in order to change the outcomes of your goals. You are truly the only one who can easily make your success goals reality. Other people may guide you, but at the end of the day, the life journey on that path of success is yours alone to take. This book is simply a guide along that path; one that will empower you for your ability to succeed.

What inspired me to write this book?

Inspiration for this book came to me as I discovered myself repeating the same concepts to my clients, while I helped them lose weight, succeed in their career goals, or heal from chronic diseases naturally.

It is a rule of mine that no matter what success or health goal we want to achieve, there are always solutions hidden in our lives, and environments to help us get there.

I always give my clients very simple explanations regarding their body's physiology, and tell them that there is a hidden wisdom resident within everyone's bodies. Then, it dawned on me that I could put all that wisdom into a book to help everyone to succeed in their lives.

If my clients could make better life choices based on information they were taking away from our sessions, then it made sense that others could also benefit from reading these concepts.

Self Mastery For Success is a way to reunite us with the understanding we are all in the same boat when it comes to our health. We all have struggled with one health issue or another.

The need to lose weight is as common a denominator as a cold. All of us who tried so many different ways to get healthy know what a daunting task it can be to keep trying to lose it, while stuck at the same weight, or it could be even worse… gaining weight instead of losing.

The same concern applies to other forms of success that we try so hard to achieve in life, only to end up with greater failures.

This book is for all those who never really learned how to succeed. Everyone has an idea of what it is, but we do not have a clue on how to attain it and keep it in our daily, busy, stressed and hectic lives. We often disassociate ourselves from success, as if it were "out there" or a "too hard, not for me" thing. Some of us have not learned that being successful, healthy, and living at our ideal weight is not a privilege for only a few, but **it is our birthright to have**! In simple terms – **You Were Born To Win!**

This book is for all who are expected to know far more than they know, and really need to know how to access success. If there is a vulnerable person freaking out about their lack of success, this book will change rapidly and dramatically their circumstance.

In the past, these folks did not know what to do and often have settled for less. That's ok, that's in the past – and remember it's never too late to turn your life around for the better.

CHAPTER 1

Your Healthy Success Image

Your brain and your nervous system control your:

1. health
2. wellness
3. success
4. and everything else about you!

Your brain and nervous system control your entire body, and you express yourself through your body. There are two systems expressing through your brain and nervous system:

1. the autonomic system
2. the central nervous system

Your autonomic nervous system is automatic and unconscious, functioning without your awareness. It controls your:

1. respiratory system
2. circulatory system
3. digestive system
4. natural healing processes
5. unconscious beliefs about success
6. and more..

Your central nervous system controls your:

1. decision-making
2. walking
3. talking

And it controls what you do voluntarily. Your unconscious mind will be discussed later in the book. Let's have a look at how your central nervous system affects your health and success.

Your brain uses five senses, or sensing systems, to position you into your world, and to help you make accurate decisions to help you adjust to your success. These senses are:

1. sight (vision)
2. smell (olfactory)
3. taste (gustation)
4. hearing (audibility)
5. touch (tactile)

These five senses provide information to your brain about the world you live in; then, your brain makes decisions based on that information, and what is already stored from your prior experiences too.

For example, if your nose smelled something burning and/or your eyes saw a fire... your brain would command your whole body to move away from the danger. All of this is based on what is happening during the period and space right here and right now. Moreover, it is highly based on what has been stored in your memory about the potential damage of fire.

Simply, your brain commands your body to do something or to change something, based on the information it has and it receives. Basically, your body's functioning is indirectly influenced by what is happening in your world.

Out of the five senses that influence the information to the brain, **your vision dominates the rest**! What you see is much more powerful than you know. In fact, some scientists now believe that the nerve that supplies the retina of the eye could be a direct outgrowth of the brain, as it is so clearly favored. This is because vision dominates the brain, out of all the five senses put together.

An example to prove to you that your brain favors visual information, is to ask yourself this question, "What does a strawberry taste like?" or "What does the ocean sound like?" You will quickly notice that long before you could recall the taste of the strawberry, you brought up the image of the strawberry. Your brain showed you a picture of that nice strawberry you once saw and had stored a picture of it in your brain. Then, you brought up the taste of it.

Similarly, with the ocean, you first saw the beautiful blue ocean on a wonderful island. Then, you heard the peaceful sound of the ocean waves.

My point is that you must be very careful of the images you feed into your brain, as they are crucial to how your brain and your nervous system command and run your body and your life. Images/pictures get stored in your brain very quickly, and influence your thinking much more than the other four senses. Because your brain favors vision in making decisions about your health and your life, keep a close watch on what you are allowing yourself to see on TV, at the movies, at events, etc.

Stop and ask yourself this vital question: How often do you feed your brain pictures that say I'm overweight, or diseased, or a failure, and struggling? We all have a mental picture of what we think:

1. we look like
2. we behave like
3. and we live like.

This is called our **self-image**. We also have a picture concept of how others see us as well. This concept is often very different from what we think we are like. Often, the image that we have of ourselves is much worse than what others actually see in us.

Sadly, we have stored so many images representing poor reference points of ourselves, and we compare ourselves to others. We compare ourselves to what we see in the world around us. Yes, we have this tendency to exaggerate the image of things we do not like about ourselves. We do this because often, we think that we have so many things that we don't like.

Sometimes, we will panic over gaining a little weight (a pound or ten). This produces horrible images of permanent obesity and failure, and then stores them in our sub-conscious mind.

Those images become how we start seeing ourselves. We see images of ourselves being so grossly obese that we cannot fit through the door! We see images of failure, poverty, struggle, and we tend to minimize images of success, or see only success in other people and maximize that.

How often have you complimented a friend saying they look good, and yet they don't believe it because they have a picture stuck in their mind of looking like an elephant instead.

At the same time, maybe you cannot accept a compliment from another person because of a deeply stored image of yourself. We all can relate to that. I had a time in my life when I saw myself as obese as a sumo wrestler! One of my doctor friends heard me talking about how fat I was, and was shocked. She saw me in a very different light than I saw myself.

She saw me as a beautiful and curvy woman instead! How bizarre is that? She said that she would have loved to have a body as curvy as mine! We both had different images of what I looked like! I was shocked to hear that others admired my body, when all I saw in myself was a failure.

I had seen myself as obese for so long that it had become my self-concept. From that day, I started changing my self-image. I started picturing my sexy curves instead of seeing that humongous body image!

I have a personal rule against saying anything bad about my body, even if I gain weight. *It is a great success strategy to say positive and encouraging things about your body.*

> *Now my mother thinks I compliment myself too much!*
> This just might be a sign of approaching success.

When we think of ourselves, we think in pictures as well. It is a natural tendency to create the picture of success or failure to match what we think of ourselves. Unfortunately, we often pick the worst picture and assign it as an image of our success.

Then, we look for ways to validate that worst picture of ourselves repeatedly, based on that belief. We may point to the evidence, to our fat waistlines, fat arms, "thunder thighs," or our every past failure. Once we have accepted and validated those images long enough, we make it a habit that occurs automatically.

This negative image often comes with deep and strong emotions like hate, disgust, shame, and guilt, which plant that self-image even deeper into our memories. Focus on that poor self-image long enough, and it will become your set point for the rest of your life. You will always see a version of that image every time you look at the mirror, or when anyone pays attention to your body or to your successes.

There Is Never Enough

Some will never accept that they have enough money in their lives. This happens because their set point is one of struggle and poverty. This is why people are discovering that they are self-sabotaging their progress. It is because their lives do not match their self-image of personal poverty and struggle, even when others see them differently.

When someone else's image of you does not match your set point image in your brain, you tend to reject all positive compliments, or minimize them to make them less effective. This, again, helps you validate that poor self-image you hold of yourself, so that you can continue to see yourself as a loser, failure, or as obese. This is how you chose to see yourself, even if others do not see you that way.

As you continue to validate that loser image of yourself, it will grow and persist until it solidifies into reality. There is a saying. "What you focus on repeatedly will persist." That is just how it is.

This applies to health and illness as well

Once a person has received the diagnosis of a disease in their body, human nature is that they tend to start referring to themselves in terms of that disease, and only that. Much of the time, I saw that once a patient has been diagnosed with diabetes, high blood pressure, or gout, it is almost like a permission slip to change their image into that new identity. They tend to form a solidified image in their brain of being diabetic or hypertensive for the rest of their lives!

When you hold the image of sickness, continuously identifying yourself as the disease long enough, it becomes harder to heal from that disease. It becomes a part of your identity. How can you self-heal from something that has become you? **I am not saying to ignore your diseases or diagnosis!**

All I am saying is that your whole being is not diseased; rather, just a small part. In the case of diabetes, your pancreas is sick; the rest of your systems are functioning properly. When you focus on the parts of yourself that are well, you are able to feed images of health into your memory. Having healthy images of yourself in your brain will promote more healing commands from your brain to your body to heal.

This will lead to a healthier condition of your body, which then promotes increased healing of the diabetes in the pancreas.

As I said, we live in a world where people identify their whole body as being diseased by that one condition. This gives the wrong image to your brain. In turn, your brain commands more disease to the body because that is what you have chosen to see yourself as being, sick. **Always be very careful of how you identify yourself... you are influencing your body's functioning!**

The same thing can be said about failure

We often tend to identify ourselves, our whole being, as a failure just because we have failed in one area of our lives. How many of us give up on our bodies because we failed on yet another fad diet?

Our entire self-esteem suffers because of one failed fat diet! Can you believe it? Your brain thinks in images fed by your thoughts, or whatever you see around you. You have an image of everything in your world, be it your body size, your failures, your diseases, whatever.

When you have a new goal to change anything in your life, you MUST start choosing different images to feed your brain. This is a crucial first step, yet many of us fail to do it. Later, we wonder why we keep getting the same results, no matter what we do.

If your success goal is to lose weight and be sexier, then it is crucial that you exchange that horrible obese image you've had of yourself for decades in your brain, for one you would love to see yourself look like. It will take a few trials to get rid of that old set point image of you, but persistence is the key. You must do this first before you even choose what kind of diet to try this time.

Use whatever technique you know to change that image. Remember that out of all your five senses, your brain favors vision. Therefore, the best way to influence your success most rapidly is to change your set point self-image.

As you set your new success goal, you must guard and protect those images you are feeding your brain. You also must constantly oppose the stored images that will come up. If you decide to change any set pattern in your life, you will always provoke internal resistance. Just wait for it! Boom...

Tips:

Here are a few techniques I teach my clients to imagine themselves healthier and thinner. Take time to do this daily, and add as many details as possible each time.

Technique 1)

If your goal is weight loss:

Stand in front of a full-length mirror and outline the edge of your body. Now, imagine yourself shrinking into the new and thinner you. Next, draw another outline of your shrunken body. What you are doing is drawing your thinner self as you want to be, within the outline of your overweight self. You quickly notice that the thinner, sexier you, is already within you. It is already there, not out there somewhere. Your thinner you is already within you!

This exercise helps you understand that losing weight and becoming sexy is an inside job! It shows a new possibility to your mind. This technique works quite fast, and is better than months and months of psychotherapy. **We all suffer from a little self-image distortion.**

If your goal is success:

Stand in front of the mirror and see yourself already being a success. If you want to be rich, then just see yourself already wearing richer persons' clothing, having your hair cut and styled as the rich do. See yourself in your new rich person's home... in your rich person's bathroom, and look at the wealthy, successful image reflecting back at you.

While standing there, contemplate what your rich self looks like on the other side of the mirror, what they will be doing on a typical day, and what will excite them. Imagine those things, and while you do... start to feel the emotions and excitement that the rich version of yourself would be feeling on any day in front of the mirror.

I ask my clients to think of problems and solutions that their richer self would think of. They might think of problems such as:

1. which investment to get involved with
2. whether to sell the yacht and buy a new one
3. whether to add a second garage to the house or not
4. which country to take the kids on holiday
5. etc...

Always show your brain new possibilities so it can create fresh reference points.

To achieve your success goal you have to SEE it as if it were already obtained. Images are powerful to your brain, and your brain creates your body and your life.

Technique 2)

Power of self-photos:

Find old photos of yourself (when you were happier, more excited about life, and slimmer than you are now) all over the house. Make sure to put them by the mirrors in your bathroom, or use them as your computer and cell phone wallpaper. The vital point here is to put the photos in places where you look at frequently.

It is easier to believe yourself than to believe other people.

If you can have photos of yourself looking the way that you would love to look again, then using those photos will be very effective. Childhood pictures have innocence, fun and happiness. These pictures all over your house will trigger a sense that 'life is good', and it can be better. Besides, it puts a smile on your face to remember old childhood stories!

If weight loss is your goal, then I suggest you search for photos of the slimmest you, and place them around your home.

Technique 3)

Admiration power:

Cut out a photo of a successful person, or a celebrity whom you admire and put your photo next to them or on top of them. This technique works well for people who don't have photos of themselves looking thinner and sexier, or do not have many childhood photos.

Have fun while doing this. If it is not your thing, then just have the celebrity's photo in your home for inspiration. These are only examples I give my clients, and they take them or come up with their own. Just have fun with it!

There are so many ways to do these techniques. Every person is different and can come up with ideas of how to use the techniques! The whole point here is to have your brain change from 'I am always overweight and ugly' to 'actually I can be successful and slimmer too'. Remember, your brain believed what it saw as yourself before. It is really up to you to change your self-image set point. Every little thing you do counts towards achieving your goal or not achieving it.

This is not to disillusion your brain.

These techniques are a new way to focus on results, rather than on your feared image that governed you for so long. This is a doorway to an acceptable self-image. Once you have that improved self-image, you will start to get excited about who you are, your own body, and who you are about to become. You will start to appreciate yourself and slowly, little by little, you will start to fall in love with the new you. Look at a picture of yourself as small child or as a baby from time-to-time. This is simply to remind you of your own innocence, and to remember that once in your life you were just 'you' without all the complications.

This is something that can be used for any new success goal you want to achieve. You must always be humbled in your success goals. A photo of you as an innocent child does the trick quickly. My baby photos go on my fridge every time I set up a new goal for myself. I stare at them and am in awe of how innocent life is without all the complications.

Humility is an important thing to have in this world. My clients tell me that this baby picture technique works for them for humility, because it connects to your subconscious mind and is beyond the understanding of your conscious mind. So, just do it! If it is not for you, then try something else to bring humility into your success goal.

Whatever you want to achieve always can be done in a humble way.

Your health and your success

Frequently, we don't realize that keeping healthy is one of our most successful states of being. Health and success go together in a synergetic manner, as they have similar energies.

One of the biggest success secrets today is to have the habit of a health routine. This is noticeable throughout history and in all successful people. Look at accomplished athletes, movie stars, millionaires, CEOs, etc. They all have some form of health routine that complements their success. They have all the health and success routines joined together to gain more success in a shorter time with less struggling.

Examples of routines include:

1. playing golf weekly
2. eating healthy food regularly
3. being punctual
4. exercising
5. working harder
6. being focused
7. exercising with a personal trainer

You will find that mix of health and success routines in successful people more than in those who are unsuccessful.

Am I saying that healthy routines are vital to success? Not necessarily, I am challenging you to observe the two routines in action, as they work together towards your prosperity. You can make your own conclusion, of course.

It will be hard not to notice the obvious association between health and success routines, as you engage in them together. You can also see it the other way around. When people decide to take charge of their health, they tend to attract more success in other areas of their lives as well, as compared to those who remain unhealthy.

Being fit and healthy increases the flow of positive energy in your body, in your life, and into your own being. Being successful also tends to increase the flow of positive energy through your body and your life. Health and success work well together as they increase your life energy.

Disease and unhealthiness in the body tend to trap your energy and prevent it from flowing easily. However, more energy flow has a synergetic effect as health increases. Healthy people tend to bring more energy into the room than unhealthy people. In a gathering of successful people, there is more positive energy than on the unemployment line.

Your health and success energy is always a part of you. Successful people have a vibrant energy, or a vibe, that is very different from those who are unsuccessful. When you walk past people, or as you communicate with them, they can sense your energy vibration, and you can sense theirs.

We often speak about it without realizing it. When someone is more successful than you are (in your judgment of them of course), you tend to feel that their energy vibe can be overwhelmingly attractive and intriguing to you. This can pull you towards wanting to do better for yourself and to mimic their success.

The same applies to someone who is fitter and/or healthier than you are. They have a stronger vibration that is attractive, and it motivates you. This pulls you towards wanting to do something about improving your health and reducing weight.

However, the opposite can happen too. You might be negatively overwhelmed by the success of others. Their higher energy might repel you so much that it discourages you completely from attempting to succeed. Their energy of success can trigger your fears and inadequacies, which can push you to withdraw into defeatist mentality. Unsuccessful people are often scared off by others' success vibration. It is easier to hang around with others who have a similar (and therefore, lower) vibration, than to have to face the challenge of being successful.

Healthy people tend to scare off unhealthy people in a similar way. The energy vibration of health and success just do not align with those of unhealthy and unsuccessful people. Subconsciously, we attract people whose energy vibrations match our own.

We live in a world where many people have forgotten what it is like to live life feeling alive and vibrant! Today's world has so many distractions and issues that vibrant living has stopped to exist as the norm. It has been replaced by surviving! Many people just survive from day to day, and this seems to be the status quo! We do not move forwards towards what we want, we stay stuck and stagnate while allowing time to pass by. There is a lot of comfort in stagnation. When people do rise up and move forward it is a shock to the rest of the population, because they were expected to stagnate just like everybody else.

When you think about it, we live, and we discuss our own un-healthiness and our failures daily, rather than encourage each other to push forward towards health and success.

Success and health are the birthright for everyone; they are simply your forward journey from point A to point B. Point A is where you are right now, and point B is where you want to be in your life, a place that allows you to be alive and vibrant. Prosperity is the measurement of that systematic forward movement towards your goal, which leads you to that success.

Is it easy to be prosperous? No, it is just worth it! Prosperity is a state that increases the energy flow in you, as you keep advancing towards your success goal. When you look at someone you consider prosperous, you can sense that positive energy flow through him or her. As human beings, we have the ability to sense anyone's energy flow, either positive or negative. We call it "a vibe," and what we sense is the actual energy flowing through their beings – whether positive or negative.

Energy is energy - it is only the flow of energy carrying either the positive or the negative feelings. Have you ever noticed that when you are around some people, it feels like an iceberg just smashed into the earth?

If you were in a social setting, where people are having a great time and laughing, and these negative people walk into the room... doesn't the mood change when they walk in? It is amazing, isn't it? You notice their "negative vibe," and you just feel something is not right with them. **Actually, you KNOW something is not right with them.**

Still, many of us pursue goals or chase after success, and sacrifice our health in the process. When we work long hours and do not give the body the exercise, nutrition, and the rest it needs to be healthy, we are sacrificing everything. If we spend all of our time chasing a dream, and forget to exercise our bodies, which we normally do, it is downright dangerous for our health. By denying our health needs to chase our dreams, we make the journey toward prosperity long and hard, instead of an easy ride.

When you incorporate health goals into your journey to prosperity, you gain momentum. You have merged two similar energies that energize you even more. The two energies together propel you with so much power and force, that success has no alternative but to manifest inevitably.

Remember that everything in your life is energy.
This is a scientific fact.

Prosperity is the forward movement towards your success goal. Prosperity is the symbol of the journey you take, that builds up on top of itself, (piles of money), and the positive energy that propels you ahead. Everything on your path, the path of your prosperity journey, is nourished throughout all your life in that way.

There will be no goal to achieve that will act in isolation. Those goals will constantly be supported (or opposed) by the other major areas of your life. Whether your success goal is physical, like losing weight (and dropping four sizes), or a mental goal like always having more confidence, or a spiritual goal (such as learning to love yourself), you are still involved and influenced by all the other areas in your life.

Failure and Lack involve all major areas in life

Failure or lack of prosperity always involves the major areas of your life. There are constantly deeper reasons as to why you are not prospering, and these go beyond the obvious physical reasons.

Many do not understand there is a root cause of their failures, which could involve their mental processes, or emotional root causes. You must realize the role their environment plays in the destruction of their dreams. This is also possible – that there are spiritual routes blocking dreams from manifesting.

Usually, humans only look at the physical facts in front of them, assuming that the problem is just the way it is. People do not see the underlying self-sabotaging that goes on in our mindsets and in our habits, which dominate our lives.

Plant Your Seed of Success

Every success goal, related to health or anything else in life, that you can perceive in your mind (as an image or picture) is already planted as a seed thought. A dream of having an oak tree one day in the future will not manifest as an oak tree tomorrow, because it needs water, food, fertilizer, and time to prosper through its journey of becoming an oak tree.

Many of us start our journey to prosperity with a seed, and expect it to grow and be an oak tomorrow. **Prosperity does not work that way.** You do not go to the gym twice and expect six-pack abs to win a fitness contest!

You came into this world as an invisible zygote through the union of an egg and a sperm. You did not grow from a zygote, to a fetus, to an adult overnight either; it took you nine months of growth and prosperity to come into this world, and more to get to where you are today.

Whatever success goal you have for your health or prosperity is possible, and always doable. You just have to be aware of the journey that you will have to take to prosper into that success. Even a fetus in the pregnant woman's womb takes time to develop, so will your success goal take time to manifest. However, one day you WILL give birth to your success. Will it be easy to do? Nope! Giving birth is never easy. Just ask any mother out there. Is it worth it? Of course, it is!

You were meant to succeed.

Success is meant to be a part of your life, just as the sun is meant to maintain life, and oxygen is meant to keep us alive and breathing. We are designed to succeed. Success is more a part of us than anything else, and it is already present in so many other ways that we take it for granted.

Failure is what is out of place, and yet today people are more accustomed to seeing themselves as failures rather than successful. Perhaps it's because of what they see in front of them –Police and Crime Television shows, Negative World News Reports, End of the World Movies, and more. This IS what most people see, and it is often a good idea just to turn off that boob tube.

Here are five things that you need to adjust to having your success goals manifest. They include your:

1) **Thoughts** – These are ideas that open your eyes to the opportunities around you. Success happens with what little is around you. Look and see what you have. What can you do with it? How much of a difference can you make to someone's life? People have created major success just from using what was available to them. Examples are Donald Trump, Tony Robbins, and Richard Branson.

    We live in two worlds, the world of thought (our inner world) and the physical world. The two worlds are separate, distinct, yet they inter-exist. One creates the other. You are constantly thinking good thoughts and bad thoughts, productive thoughts and non-productive thoughts. You will never stop thinking; you just need to be more aware and more in control over your thoughts. Thought control, your own self-thought control is the first step to manifesting success or failure in your life. How you think will determine your ultimate outcome.

2) **Emotions** – These are the crucial feelings that connect you to your abilities. Emotions create chemical shifts in your body that raise your awareness. They provoke pictures that when

coupled with your feelings and imagination inspire and make you unstoppable.

3) **Actions** – These actions you take create the world around you. Look at buildings, roads, etc. Someone took action and created them. Look at yourself. What you are today is a result of the actions you took in the past.

4) **Persistence** – When you are going with the flow and fast turbulence comes at you, do not jump off. Just hold on tight and keep going. Remember that it is often the last key on the key ring that opens the door.
As a child is being born, we, in the medical field, know that when labor pains become faster and stronger, the baby is about to be delivered. Do not give up. When the going gets tough… get tougher. Stay on the path toward your success goal. Persistence is the key.

5) **Momentum** - This stage is the precursor to success. Once momentum has set in, then your success is inevitable. You are almost there. It is already a done fact! Success is at the next corner. So relax!

CHAPTER 2

The Spirit of Success

Raison D'Etre – A Reason for Being

Have you ever stopped to think that you had a purpose or a reason for being on this planet at this time? Why are you alive now while others are not? Why do you have a human body? Does your body also have a purpose on this planet?

Your body's job is to take care of yourself and provide a vessel for you as a being, to live in. Do you agree that you, as a human being, are so much more than just your body?

You are bigger than your body, your mind, and your soul.

Your life is a summation of many aspects of you, co-existing. These aspects are:

- the physical
- the mental
- the emotional
- the environmental
- the spiritual life

Your physical body is the only part of you that is truly visible and tangible; it is just a small part. Even though many of us only identify ourselves by our bodies and our physical aspects, there is so much more than that to us as human beings.

Your physical aspect is the way you express yourself and the way you manifest your life on earth. However, YOU, yourself, are a sum of all those aspects: physical, mental, emotional, environment, and spiritual... and you are actually an INFINITE being. You are more than physical:

- Because you have abundant and intangible parts.
- You have a wonderful soul and an amazing spirit.
- Your body serves you because without it, you would be invisible, intangible, and inaudible.

You would not be able to feel the sunlight, taste delicious foods, or feel the tenderness of a gentle touch. Your body is part of your divine self. If you cannot love it for what it is - at least love it for what it allows you to do here on earth... to learn to succeed.

Spiritual Health

Spiritual health involves knowing yourself as a human being, and knowing your creator. This has nothing to do with any religion. My aim for adding this part is not to preach dogma or guilt, control, or manipulation. It is totally the opposite. It's for you to appreciate who you are as a human being. Spiritual health is about unifying the totality of you, and not separating into your aspect parts.

It is about being the YOU you came to earth to be...the WINNER... and somehow you got too distracted by failures and struggling to remember. Spiritual health is about respecting all forms of spiritualties and religions, judging none. Whatever people believe in is up to them, and whatever you believe in is up to you. Spiritual health is about pure energy that loves all that is and judges nothing.

Spiritual health is about connecting more to who you truly are and what your real purpose in life is here on Earth. It is connecting and knowing your Creator, no matter what you believe created and made you. It is about knowing and connecting back to your Creator, and the guidance your creator provides.

You are the precursor to it all

Knowing who you truly are... is the precursor to success and good health. Spending time getting to know YOU, the person who you really are, is so important for your prosperity. This is not done very often these days. We just don't spend enough time with ourselves to know who we really are. It is easier to go along with the idea of what others think of us, than to spend time with ourselves.

How could you know if the person you know yourself to be is the true you, if you don't invest the time in getting to know yourself? You may have a very superficial knowledge of yourself. How could you possibly succeed in life if you have no clue as to who you really are?

People have a tendency to take the identity that society and others put on them, rather than seek their true identity, which can be distant from who they really are.

> *"As I began to know me for who I truly am, I became very different from the person I thought I used to be."*

Was it easy to get to know me?

No, but it was just worth it. Because having the wrong identity can cause many confusions, inadequacies, trust issues, fears, and anxieties. Understanding who you really are will help you live better and succeed faster. You get to live in congruency with your true potential, instead of existing from one identity crisis to another. You take responsibility for yourself and your actions. You will be able to stand firmly with decisions you make, knowing that they really serve you, and they are truly yours.

How can you love yourself, if you do not know yourself?

It is not surprising that we have a worldwide shortage of self-love today. It is easier to love what you know than to love what you don't know. You start to love yourself more as you get to know more about who you really are. You learn to treat yourself well, and treat your body right.

The body you live in has wisdom

It is so much more than you think it is. It has plenty of goodness in it. It means well for you. Your body will never deliberately harm you; it can only live through you. It dies if there is no soul or spirit in it. When you stop judging your body… you will be amazed at how much more wisdom it has to offer! It actually opens up a completely new mind-body-spirit connection when you stop judging and/or mistreating it.

Spiritual health involves looking after your body

Spiritual health involves looking after your mindset, and it involves looking after every single part that makes you who you really are. You are much more than what you think you are. There is so much more to you than what your conscious awareness perceives.

You were created by the same Force (God), who created everything around you. You are made to the image of that Creative Force (God) with pride and joy. You are a masterpiece in your own way.

When you look in the mirror, you see what God loves. You are made in the Creator's image and liking, whether you like yourself of not.

You are not a mistake

You were not made by mistake. It is impossible to be here in the world today and be a mistake. This Force, who has precision and perfection, created you, just like your internal systems function with precision and perfection every day.

How can God have made a mistake with you and not everyone else? How could God have created you with mistakes on the outside, if you are so perfect and precise on the inside? There is no such thing.

God is too good to single you out and punish you with ugliness! There is no fat or ugly skin that you carry around that is a mistake. Everything has its point of reference in precision and perfection, just like the beauty of nature surrounding you. Therefore, your weight gain or weight loss failed attempts are not a punishment or a mistake.

Anything you don't like about yourself can always be healed and changed back to its original state of beauty, precision and perfection, because you are a masterpiece created by the almighty God.

Your faith

Your spiritual connection relates to how you connect to your spiritual being and to the Creator. In our quest for success, we must be willing to deepen and resurrect our connection to ourselves. We are spiritual beings, and our creator gave us physical bodies and the breath of life as energy to jumpstart.

The Bible says: *"Faith is being sure of what we hope for and certain of what we do not see."*

- Hebrews 11:1

What is the point of success unless it improves upon our living experience here on this planet? Success must make you grow into more of whom you really are. It must lead you closer to your purpose here on Earth, or to discover whatever that might be.

Your success must somehow help you rise above being the people pleaser you used to be, to the self-honoring and self-respecting person you are becoming along this journey with me. Your personal success must transform you during your journey and give you a new identity that honors you.

You must be prepared to lose the old image you have carried around, as you are right now or who you were, because you are beginning a completely new journey of self-discovery.

Soon, you will create a new and reborn you at the end of your journey. This is in honor of you "The Self" and not anybody else, as it is not about them and never was. It is always just about you, only you. Your success journey is yours. Nobody else can ever walk in your success journey for you. They can walk alongside of you and support you, but they never can do your journey for you.

Opinions of Others

No one can walk the journey in your shoes, and that is the reason why the opinion of others is not your primary motivator to your success. It is merely their opinion. Only your opinion of yourself will ever transform your success journey!

It is important for you to have your own spiritual path, which is about you and your Creator during your success journey. Who you are, in your eyes and in your Creator's eyes, is crucial to succeeding at anything in life. Too often, we delete our spirituality step to pursue success goals, and we forget that self-actualization is just as important as achievement.

Success is a journey that transforms you for the better.

People may define you based on their opinion of you, but it is just an opinion. Give yourself the permission to transform and grow into a better version of you through your success process. It is *your* decision and not anyone else's.

What others think of you is actually none of your business; it is theirs. Success and failure in your life are in the hands of one person and one person alone…, and that is YOU.

Your mindset and your nervous system, which run your body and your life, are really focused on you. It doesn't matter what others and the world think or say about your goal; as long as it honors you as a human being and honors your Creator, is it worth committing to.

This may sound strange to you, but…

You have enough parts that support your success because your body is designed to succeed. There is success inside all your organ systems, as they work daily to keep you alive and well. You are made up of 47 trillion cells that work harmoniously and successfully, every single day of your life.

The only person that is strong enough to affect your nervous system and your physiology is YOU. Nothing changes in your physiology of success unless you modify your image and view of yourself.

When another calls you fat or a failure, that is his or her opinion, and nothing else, when you allow it to be registered into your nervous system. However, it has no effect in altering your physiology unless YOU agree with their opinion that you are, indeed, a failure or a fat person. The only person that can truly affect you is you. Gossip or people saying evil things about you are not strong enough to override your view of yourself, unless you allow it.

To understand this concept is life transforming. Your success depends on you and you alone. You are the architect and the creator of your success path (and if you want, your failure path).

Others can only influence you to a certain point; YOU are the one who makes the final decision, whether you agree to allow their negative view to enter your nervous system. If you allow someone's negative words and view to be validated by your nervous system, then you begin to change the self-image you have of yourself in your brain and nervous system. Once this change starts to take place, you begin to believe what others are saying, and start to create it immediately.

If their opinion were negative, such as fat and failure, you would begin to see yourself as a fat person or as a failure, and start to behave that way. This can happen instantly. You can see another walk into a room tall, happy and proud, then a change of image happens in their brain and nervous system, and that same person walks out of that room as a failure, a loser, with head held in shame.

Your words count:

You are a spiritual being, and as one, you can create your own life by what you think and what you say about yourself. The Bible *"The tongue has the power of life and death, and those who love it will eat its fruits."*

- Proverbs 18:21

Since that is reality, be very careful with what you say to yourself. What you say to yourself is what matters on your success journey.

Affirmations:

You may have negative thoughts from time-to-time, but it's what you say aloud that sticks to you the quickest. This is why saying positive affirmations actively and with purpose daily is such a wonderful success routine to follow. What you will quickly notice is that you start to feel better after repeating a positive affirmation to yourself for one to two minutes. Something starts to change inside of you.

The Negative Power of Negations

A negation is a negative affirmation. Unfortunately, for many years, the majority of us have been using the power of negative affirmations in our lives. We have been trained, or have mistakenly trained ourselves, to use the negative affirmation power rather than a positive and constructive affirmation.

Somehow, we have learned to honor and value things like mediocrity, poverty and failure, more than to respect riches and success. We affirm negativity daily more than positivity. Do a checkup (from the neck up) on this. You'll be amazed of how often you negatively comment on yourself, the conditions of your life and environment, than think positively about it. It's simply amazing!

When you were young...

Young kids, including you and me, watch movies where the bad guys, who were mean and evil, were often extremely rich with tons of money. Movies tend to be hypnotic, and all of us were brainwashed that being rich was evil. Thus, we unconsciously affirmed poverty rather than riches, just like the hero of the movie.

Now, we SAY things like:

- oh, poor thing, or
- I can't afford anything, or
- I am not good enough

These are also favorite negations:

- we don't have money honey, and
- being broke

Often, society trains us to minimize ourselves when it comes to any success in our lives, and so we do that. We assume that successful people got that way via magical, yet unobtainable things as luck and good fortune, which always eluded us.

Since the average person does not feel lucky or fortunate enough, then are we to assume that we never can be successful? How can an Olympian gold medalist be a winner? Is it just by luck?

Every day, you declare what you cannot do and cannot have. The power of affirmations is always available for your success journey, so you might as well consciously use them for your own good, instead of automatically affirming that you can't, won't, don't, couldn't, shouldn't, etc..

To begin, you will want to observe yourself speaking, and adjust your words before you speak. Learn to stop when speaking negatively about your success goals. One of the best things you need to develop is your ability to keep your mouth shut, and be silent around people who are negative about anything you want to manifest in your life. Is it easy to do? Nope! We are so used to talking trash! I had to learn the hard way. As a woman it is tough to be around other women who say bad things about men and not do the same myself.

What if my deepest wish was to meet a loving and sexy man? I'd never met one because of that trashy talk. The same goes for you, men. If you talk bad about women... don't expect a good one to come into your life either.

••◆••

Your viewpoint:

Who can ever look after your success better than you?

From now on, simply don't allow yourself to say anything negative about your goals and success. It is just unacceptable, and does not help you. Don't declare how you really feel (unless it is absolutely wonderful), or how broke you are, because negative statements do not honor your success goal.

Instead, you can say how you would like things to be, and what you are doing to achieve that. Your success depends on what you say about yourself, and to yourself.

Personally, I take your success seriously enough to write a complete book to help you attain it. Since you are the only person in this whole universe who listens, every day, to what you have to say, and who has to endure the impact of your words regularly, you owe it to yourself to speak positively.

Your friends, family, and co-workers only have to listen to you for a short time, and then they get a break from your words. Guess what? You don't ever get a break from listening to yourself! You MUST listen to yourself, all day... every day. Do yourself a favor and zip-up the daily continuous flow of self-defeatist talk.

I do not think anyone could tolerate being spoken to in the manner that we sometimes speak to ourselves. With all the negative things you've said to yourself every single day, are you surprised that you have not had the success you wanted in your life? Weren't you aware that you listen to your own negativity every day?

It is not your friends who get the privilege to sit in the VIP seat of your, "I hate my life" show. You are the star, the director, and even the executive producer of your own self-talk production, and you are the audience. Yes, then you watch that show and all the reruns. This is the reason why you shouldn't ever utter a single word of negativity against yourself anymore, starting right now.

No matter how true and appropriate the negative description is to your current situation, you must find a way to define that same situation in a positive way. How do you do that? It is an acquired talent, I must admit, but eventually you will get used to transform your negative talk into beauty.

My clients practice this with me during our coaching sessions; it is really fun!

Let me give you a few examples of how to do it. If you are overweight, then don't ever confess to yourself that you are like that; instead, say:

- I am in the process of slimming my body down, or
- I am a slim person in the making, or
- I am working on my slim down project

You get the point. This is about reframing the very same thought or words without the negative connotation. Negative words, thoughts, or memories *never* help you succeed.

When you rewrite or reframe your negative thoughts and words into positive phrases, you begin healing and empowering yourself with positive talk. Another example of this relates to having no money.

Instead of declaring (with shame to yourself and others) that you are broke, instead just say that:

- I am awaiting money to come in, or
- I am waiting on money right now, or
- I am in between monies right now, or
- I am in the process of acquiring money.

If you are going through a tough situation, try saying:

- I am recovering from a tough situation.

If you are sick, then say:

- I am recovering from the flu (or cold, or whatever).

If you find yourself tired or fatigued, reframe by saying:

- I am recharging my body.

Here is an example of what you can say if you are single or divorced:

- I am open and available to meeting my ideal mate, (or the man or woman of my dreams).

Do you get that this type of declaration is considerably closer to a positive, more empowering and motivating affirmation than a negative one? In contrast to "I am broke" or "I am lazy," which are harsh and have very destructive energy attached to them, instead use a statement or declaration of transition… I am in the process of, or I am about to come into money!

No wonder people who are broke tend to recreate being broke repeatedly; that "being broke" energy is too paralyzing, and you cannot escape it…ever… with those thoughts!

The Bible states: "Beat your plowshares into swords and your prunning hooks into spears. Let the weak say I am strong" - Joel 3:10

It seems like humanity has been taught throughout history to deny the negative situations, and never to admit them. Therefore, historically, we have been taught to proclaim ONLY what we want in our lives, and never speak of what we do not want. The broke person must learn to declare that they are rich, and not to speak about being broke!

Today the norm IS a completely different ball game

Today, the norm is to speak negativity. If you eavesdrop into people's conversations, you'll find they are filled with negative proclamations about their lives. This is exactly what the great books of life warn us not to do. When you know this and pay attention to people's conversations, you'll find that not only do they declare their negative situations constantly and sometimes almost gleefully, they also compete to see who has the most horrible story to tell. You would think that there is a million-dollar prize for the worst case of mediocrity told! It is amazing to watch all of this unfold.

Oh, a word of warning here

As you remove yourself from your coffee clutches of negative talk friendships, where you are supposed to speak badly about yourself, your mate or your kids, and your life, you may attract nicknames such as "Little Miss Happy Sunshine"(and I am just saying that it may happen to you too) if you refuse to buy into their negativity. Just smile, knowing that your life IS changing rapidly for the better, and that their stupid nicknames are a miniscule price to pay to keep your path to success clean and clear! Don't you think? If push comes to shove, you can always find new and more successful friends.

Develop the habit of affirming goodness

How do you get into the habit of affirming only good and positive things to yourself and about yourself? It is not that easy, but not that hard. The straight answer is you do it consciously and deliberately.

Affirming good things just doesn't come naturally, or on a silver platter. There is no one on the planet that has that natural talent. It is acquired, and you get it… the hard way, with lots of daily practice.

I wish I could say that you could be brainwashed and become positive overnight, but that is not an option, although we all wish there was. Once you have acquired the skill of affirming your good (that means affirming the good you desire in your life), you become a natural at it. Then, it becomes part of your life.

Remember, however, that as human beings we have a natural tendency toward negative self-talk than positive. So don't expect positive self-talk to occur by osmosis, while you just lie there doing nothing to make it occur. You'll have to focus on the task and work on it.

Learn to catch yourself mid-speech.

You'll soon catch yourself resorting to old negative self-talk, but stop mid-sentence, and then go in the positive direction. All you have to do is gently return to positive every time you derail. Do not give up on yourself, as it does take a while to get the momentum of positive self-talk going, and once you have momentum you have won the race.

Just remember that what you say about yourself and what you say to yourself is what sticks most in your nervous system, and attracts situations that will validate what you are saying to yourself and about yourself.

Have you noticed that what people say about themselves has a magical way of happening to them? People who talk prosperity to themselves, and about themselves, tend to have prosperity in their lives. People who talk poverty to themselves and about themselves tend to be broke all the time, and seem to attract more poverty into their lives.

Luck...

What about those that practically self-talk themselves into having bad luck?

> *"Born under a bad sign,*
> *I have been down since the day I began to crawl,*
> *If it wasn't for bad luck,*
> *I wouldn't have any luck at all."*

Albert King wrote it, Cream sang it, and most us tend to live it because of our failure to control our negative voice. And some people tend to be unlucky even in lucky situations, don't they?

If you are one of those people, I challenge you to keep training yourself to speak only positively to yourself and imagine abundance in your new picture from this day forwards.

Creating your destiny

It takes a while to figure out that you are the creator of your good fortune, and your bad fortune too. We often take pride and honor in our good achievements, but tend to run away from negative achievements and rapidly point fingers at other to blame them. We quickly forget about the role we play in creating our misfortunes. We magnify everybody's part in it, and we tend to minimize our own.

To be the creator of your own destiny, you must learn to take responsibility for your life in its entirety. Responsibility includes everything, the good and the bad. It means that you examine a situation and notice the part that you played in it.

It is not easy to see your role in the creating of your misfortune. It's so much easier to point the finger of blame at another. Even though taking responsibility for any negative misfortune in your own life is hard to do, it's also the most liberating experience to own being at cause and responsible.

Taking responsibility gives you a chance to make things right. You don't run away from issues; instead, you get the opportunity to rectify the wrong and make better choices. You get to alter the path and steer yourself back to success.

What is the best way to create the life you want?

If I told you that your words are as prophecy to your future, would that help? Do you want to know where your life will be in 5, 10 or 20 years from now? Well, just listen very carefully to what you are saying to and about yourself. What you declare into your life will become your reality.

You already know how to create your life; you've done it every day. Where your life is today is exactly where you have been prophesizing it would be for the past 5 -10 years.

Flipping decisions?

You know there are some people who would say one thing to one person and the opposite to another. Either way, they are creating their future reality, albeit a more confusing one.

Create your own reality

You are the one who can create any kind of life you want. You can go anywhere; you can be anything, do anything and have anything you want. You were born with unlimited possibilities and potentials, and they are still within you. You must believe in yourself, declare it, and be on the side that is cheering you on to victory. Be on your own team; be your personal cheerleader. Be there for yourself.

Do not work against yourself

You already have enough things working against you, including other people, circumstances, negative thoughts, criticism by others, and jealousy. The last thing you need in your life is to be against yourself. It's just as wrong to criticize yourself as it is to criticize others. You are a masterpiece of Creation, made by the wisest, powerful and generous Creator, to have the most vibrant and abundant life possible.

What if I did everything wrong until now?

Who hasn't? Every day, you and I have a new chance to make things right with ourselves and within our lives. It is better to walk alongside yourself in your journey of success than to be your own opponent.

Sure, you may have areas you need to improve in your life, as we all do; however, that doesn't mean that you need to be hard on yourself. Self-love and compassion go a long way.

Learn to be kind and loving towards your own self. As I said, you already have so much against you in this world that you must focus on taking care of yourself. Kindness to yourself will lead you to an easier and simpler life.

Being harsh, mean, and unkind to yourself can only lead you to hardship. No matter what you have done in the past to yourself, you don't need to abuse yourself over it. It is so easy to be kind to yourself. All you need is five minutes in the morning when you wake, and make intentional positive self-talk declarations about yourself that empower you, like:

- I have great eyes
- I am a good and loving person
- I am grateful that I am walking with both legs today
- My arms can hold a cup of tea, and I am thankful for that
- I am a beautiful child of a wonderful and perfect God
- My body is the loving vessel of God's kindness
- and more.

Not only for women…

That is what it takes to be on your side, and it's even more effective if you do it in front of the mirror, watch yourself speak, and notice your facial expressions.

Some of my female clients have never told themselves that they are beautiful. Isn't it strange that women often wait for men to tell them that? Even so, women hardly say it to themselves, if at all. Mostly, we focus on our faults, and compare ourselves to others.

> "…If you compare yourself to others,
> you may become vain and bitter;
> for always there will be greater and
> lesser persons than yourself."
>
> — Max Ehrmann, Desiderata:
> A Poem for a Way of Life

I've seen women use the mirror as an excuse to criticize rather than admire themselves. We've all seen women put on layers of make-up to hide flaws, and that often works well, but at the same time also secretly feeds their insecurities.

As a woman, I know that we have trained ourselves to see only what needs to be fixed, and that makes self-appreciation such a strange practice. It took me a little while to acquire the habit of… first, appreciating my natural face before I put any makeup on it. I teach my clients to develop the same habit too.

I don't oppose the use of make-up, but I believe in self-appreciation and gratitude FIRST, before hiding away the flaws. I believe we are spiritually beautiful just the way that our creator made us. Everyone has his or her own unique beauty and should proclaim it daily. You are beautiful just as you are!

You are awesome, wonderful, and beautifully created just the way you are. You have the power to be amazing and beautiful any time you chose. Do not give up that power. Do not doubt yourself and never be against yourself. You and only you have the power to create yourself the way you want to be, and create the life you want. It can be a great and enjoyable journey to success if you continuously declare it. Guard what comes out of your mouth as you walk towards it on your path to success.

Talk of your life becoming better.

Don't speak about your life as it is right now, but speak about what you desire from life and how it is becoming better for you. Never speak about things that do not lead to your success.

Creating a Success Mindset
Just Takes Some Simple
Mental Adjustments

CHAPTER 3

Mindset success power

From this book, I want you to take away knowledge of yourself and your body, seeing both in a different light so that you can make new choices that empower you.

Stop beating yourself up or blaming yourself

To begin with, you must stop beating yourself up for past failures, whether it just happened today, or it's happened in the past, just let it go! You are not unlucky or a victim of poor choices. You cannot blame genetics or anything else. Self-blame does not lead to anything positive for anyone. It never has and never will. It is one of the most futile things you can spend your energy doing. The longer you blame yourself, or blame someone or something else, the longer it will take you to learn your lessons from that failure and get back on your path to success. Too many people beat themselves up repeatedly, over the failure of one thing or another, wasting precious energy and momentum to create success!

The one way to learn from our failures is by taking responsibility for our own actions and creations. You must get to a point where you see and accept responsibility for the role you played in past failures. It can be a harsh reality to accept, but you gain an incredible personal power in doing so.

After taking responsibility for past failures, you'll realize that there were some situations in which you could have made better choices, and you now know that, and you also know which choices you could have made instead. With this knowledge, you can start to formulate new steps and actions to ensure that these failures do not happen again.

Self-blame is totally wrong ...

This is how powerful and crucial taking personal responsibility for your progress is. We often fear taking responsibility, but there is not one instance to justify self-blame, in any aspect of your life. The decision to let go of blaming yourself will change your life **forever** for the better. Be careful not to start feeling sorry for yourself in the process of accepting responsibility for your past failures, such as weight loss attempts.

What comes after blame is guilt, anger or shame?

You can deal with these emotions by focusing on the lessons you've learned and how you'll make different choices in the future. Seeing the good in everything that has happened to you allows you to begin to turn everything around. I believe that in every negative situation or event in your life, there is a secondary positive situation to discover.

The problem with blaming yourself is that once you have done it, and repeated it for a while, it soon becomes a habit, which leads to a new self-limiting belief. When you have a new self-limiting belief, it forms a negative self-image mental picture, and that image is loaded deeply into your brain and nervous system.

This negative self-image becomes your new identity, and is the one that starts to govern your future decisions about taking actions to fulfill your success goals. It's not very wise to operate this way.

Busy, busy, busy ...

Your mind is always busy, busy, busy... thinking about things. That is what it does. Your mental chatter is always on. Sometimes you are aware of it, sometimes you are not. You have those moments when you catch yourself thinking about something, and you wonder, 'why in the world am I thinking that?'

Sadly, you cannot stop yourself from this automatic thinking all day; it is impossible. When you meditate, you can stop it for a short time. As soon as you finish meditating, you continue hearing that voice inside your head again. When internal thoughts get out of hand, they can create low-grade stress with no real cause.

It is a battlefield for your thoughts

Do not leave your thoughts rambling on unconsciously as this is detrimental to your success and health. Your mind is a battlefield where all sorts of thoughts are fighting, trying to overtake if you do not protect and defend your pathway to success. You want to minimize mental activities that lead to a stressful internal environment because it will manifest physically.

An overactive mind can quickly deplete your energy and lead to physical exhaustion, plus mental and emotional exhaustion. You can end up with low energy levels because of continual uncontrolled mental activities. This lack of mental control only promotes stress, because it has become a negative ingrained habit, hard to shed.

One of these useless mental activities is *worry*.

To worry about things only depletes your energy levels without giving you a solution to try out. It is better to take a stand and do something about any situation instead of worrying about it all day.

And... Stress isn't that good either

Stress is not good for your body. No matter how small your worry is, your body will activate a stress response as if your life is being threatened.

Have you noticed that when you are in a stressful situation, you do not feel well about anything else? How can you possibly focus on success or looking good if you don't feel good? The other sad thing about stress is that it is the root cause of so many diseases in your body. Living under stress makes your body feel uneasy; it has to work harder just to help you heal. If you continue along *this* path, you might start suffering from organ diseases, as organs become exhausted.

Your mind may get used to the stressful life and not take any notice. However, your body will never get used to the continuous stress you are experiencing. It will never adapt to your stressful lifestyle. It will constantly look for ways to get rid of that stress for you. Your body reacts every time and exhausts your stored energy physically, mentally, and emotionally.

Your body perceives stress as a life-threatening danger

This is due to the way it attacks your organ systems, and because of the fear behind most stresses, your body reacts by activating its protective mechanisms. Look at what happens to you when you are stressed:

- Your heart rate increases.
- Your stomach goes into knots.
- Your pupils dilate.
- Your breathing is disturbed and becomes uncontrollable.
- You become pale and clammy.

A body that is continuously responding to the internal triggers of stress doesn't have any energy left to heal itself or rebuild its muscles. This leads to the weakening of your immune and digestive systems. With a weakened immune system, you get sick easily. With a weakened digestive system, you gain weight easily.

Fight or flight is our survival-instinct mechanism

It was created millions of years ago to keep you safe from that Saber Tooth Tiger and out of other dangerous situations. It has filtered down through the millennia into your 21st century body.

The Fight or flight response gives you only two options to deal with stress. One is super-human strength to fight off your opponent, so your body does not get hurt. The other is to give you super speed to run for your life and escape the danger that may bring you severe harm or death. This mechanism is the best thing that ever happened to us, as it is our own natural survival instinct honed to be perfect for ages.

We are designed to survive and avoid death. Therefore, during this fight or flight response, the aim is to re-direct the blood flow away from some organs into other organs that are far more critical to your survival, such as your heart and lungs. What happens is that blood flow is cut-off from the digestive and urinary systems, while it is increased dramatically to sensory organs and the musculoskeletal system.

It can be something good as well.

The fight and flight response is good for you when it happens in an appropriate manner and when it is needed. It can save your life when you are in a dangerous situation.

Stress activates the fight or flight response in your nervous system because it thinks your life is in danger. However, your body does not like being stressed all the time. The pre-nourisher need that the body has for health is actually the opposite of a stress reaction. It is… peace and tranquility.

When your pre-nourisher need for peace and tranquility is fulfilled, your health improves and your wellness prevails. Do not be fooled by someone who martyrs himself or herself with the delusion that being stressed is honorable. It is not. No part of you is designed to live under stress. You are designed to either fight it off, or flee from it.

Today in the free world, that many life-threatening situations do not exist

Thankfully, dangerous situations that people face regularly have reduced, and what remains is just low-grade stresses like:

- having a job we hate
- living life in the fast lane
- or being reachable 24/7 via emails and cell phones

Still stress is everywhere these days

Unfortunately, no matter what grade is the stress level, if your body misjudges it as threatening, it activates the same fight or flight response as in the dangerous situations. Sadly, with overstressed people this can be activated a few times a day for even the smallest of stresses.

Often, behind people's stress, lies fear. Examples are:

- the fear of missing a deadline and losing clients,
- the fear of divorce or
- the fear of being stuck in traffic.

To understand people stresses look at what fear lies behind them. If someone is stressed before an exam, they fear getting lower grades than they want. Someone may stress over giving a company presentation, making mistakes or being laughed at. It is this fear that activates the fight or flight response inappropriately.

One of the diseases of stress is headaches

There is only so much space that the brain and its covering membranes have to occupy in your skull cavity. It's a tight space. The constant increase and re-distribution of blood flow to the brain during continuous forms of low-grade stress increase pressure in the skull. Stress causes an elevation of pressure in the brain membranes and therefore, headaches.

Now, the opposite is happening to your digestive and immune systems, as they are shutting down due to restricted blood flow, you end up with stomach pains, constipation, and you become more susceptible to digestive disease. By looking deeply into how your body responds to stress, you can begin to understand why it causes or worsens so many diseases.

Short-term stress hormone

Adrenaline is the hormone released to keep you alive in times of stress. It gives us the strength to fight or run away to protect our lives and survive dangerous situations. Someone who is very active and adventurous is often called an Adrenaline Junky, and that is not far from the truth. Adrenaline Junkies produce a lot of adrenaline in their systems when doing risky, life-threatening activities.

Think of adrenaline as the short-term stress response hormone and a coping mechanism designed to cheat death. Once it's activated in the body, it acts fasts and disappears after three to five minutes. You feel the effects of adrenaline quickly when you are frightened. You react fast, then the moment passes, and you calm down.

Adrenaline is a powerful hormone that rapidly warns every cell in your body of an impending danger. This happens every time your body perceives danger, either physical or imagined. Adrenaline activates the fight or flight response and redirects all the blood flow to your critical organs. Your heart beats heavier and faster because it has more blood flowing through it. Your brain is sharper, and your five senses are on hyper-alert. Your digestive and urinary systems are on hold during this time. Your body needs an immediate increase of oxygen and energy in the form of quick available nutrition. Your metabolism speeds up to provide these.

Adrenaline activates your muscles and sets up the provision of blood flow and nutrition to supply so they contract easily. These contractions during a stress response may lead to stiffness and spasms of the neck and shoulder muscles when you have been under stress for a while.

Carbs are the best fuel during fight or flight.

The quickest energy fuel the body uses during the fight or flight response is carbohydrates, in the form of glucose (simple sugars). Glucose is easily broken down during times of crisis. It is readily liberated from its stored forms of glycogen from the liver and the muscles. Adrenaline immediately communicates to the muscles and liver to release the glycogen, which breaks down in glucose.

Then, glucose is dumped into your blood stream to be used up for energy. Fat molecules are too complex to use during stress responses. Once adrenaline has done its job, the longer-acting stress hormone called cortisol quickly replaces it.

Two long-term stress hormones

Cortisol is related to adrenaline; however, it is a longer-acting and more stable stress hormone. Your body increases the release of cortisol when there are prolonged levels of stress in your system, including physical stresses such as inflammation, or a form of mental stress as fear, anger, jealousy, or guilt.

Cortisol primarily has a protective function just like adrenaline. It also helps you mobilize glucose from your stores, which enables you to fight or run during prolonged stresses. However, it helps you to cool your body and your joints down as well, after the stress episode. It decreases inflammation in your body. This cooling effect is very soothing to those who suffer from arthritic diseases.

Cortisol, your day in and day out friend

On a daily basis, Cortisol is our friend and supports us. When you have enough cortisol in your system, you wake up in the morning as if you had a jump-start, and stay awake during the day. But when you are low in cortisol, you struggle to get up and stay up. Without sufficient cortisol, you feel like there isn't a strong enough coffee in the world to wake you up.

Cortisol levels are the highest in the mornings and as the day goes... the levels decrease. As night sets in, the levels drop, and you begin to feel sleepy. At night, another hormone called melatonin rises, as cortisol drops. This helps you to go to sleep.

Chronic stress in today's world

Today, many people live under constant stress, as we have discussed earlier. A chronic stressful lifestyle unfortunately leads to the chronic overproduction of cortisol. Remember that cortisol is meant to be produced at normal levels within the body, and to help you sustain your energy levels during the day. However, chronic stress requires a lot more stress hormone production! Therefore, your stressed-out body increases your cortisol levels to a constant extremely high level.

Look around you. Can you tell that many people live their lives secretly with long-term stress? Isn't this shocking to you?

A little stress is normal and keeps you on your toes

It is common to have a few stressful events in your life to keep you aware that life isn't always seen through rose-colored glasses. Nevertheless, it is abnormal to live life in constant stress. Prolonged stress in your body leads to negative health consequences. When you are constantly stressed, your cortisol levels are high all day, and they don't decrease at night like they should.

"I was Tossing and turning all night"

High cortisol levels in the evenings, leads to insomnia and visits to the doctor's office for prescriptions for sleeping pills. The cortisol level must drop in the evenings for your melatonin levels to rise, so that you go to sleep. Many with insomnia or challenges to sleep take sleeping tablets instead of addressing their high cortisol levels. *Remember: elevated cortisol at bedtime affects your ability to sleep.*

Poor sleep at night leads to low-grade energy levels the following day. Low energy levels always trigger increased appetite, most food consumed during that time is high carbs, and this happens because your body needs energy from foods, fast.

When you overeat or eat *too many* carbs… you gain weight.

That is one side effect of cortisol; it causes you to gain weight directly from eating. The other side effect regarding weight control is its direct effect on fat storage. *Cortisol is a fat storage hormone.* When there is an elevation of cortisol in your system, there is an increase of fat storage around your midsection.

Your body will store fat even when you do not eat much at all. That fat storage system is on full alert, so the weight will pile on faster than normal. This is why people do not lose weight, no matter how hard they try.

You cannot lose weight while your body feels that

Danger --------stress -------activates Cortisol
Starts to store energy to protect you. Your body stores energy as fat.

Often my clients say to me, "I've gained so much weight even though I am sticking to my diet. My meals are light, why I am not losing weight?" Or they might say, "This same diet worked for me before; why it isn't working for me now? I'm eating less than ever, so why is this not working?"

I tell them, "Your body will store fat if the cortisol hormone is dominant and elevated." It stores fat in your midsection and gives you that horrible belly fat look you hate so much. While people lose weight during chronic stress, what really is occurring is shocking, because their body is breaking down the proteins from within their muscles, rather than using its own supply of stored fat.

Cortisol will use glucose from the protein breakdown in muscles for energy, as it is faster and easier to access when compared to fat. Proteins are much easier to access as fuel source than fat molecules.

Therefore, when cortisol is high, fat is stored as future energy and not used for fuel. When your body thinks it's in danger and needs fuel fast, and fat metabolism takes too long, the protein from within your muscles is quickly broken down into building blocks called amino acids.

The process of muscular breakdown

Amino acids can be easily converted into glucose for fuel, and this occurs if the body's glucose store is depleted. This is how chronic stress wastes away your muscle's proteins, giving you the illusion of weight loss. These amino acids are converted to glucose through a process called glycogenesis.

A typical day

What does your typical day look like? Are you so used to your low-grade stressful life that you are not even aware of it? Here is an example of how a typical day looks for the average client that I treat:

1. It starts with the person stressing about their next day before that day has even begun.

2. They think about their next day the night before and then go to bed stressed about it.

3. The alarm clock goes off, and the person has that "oh my God NO" attitude since the beginning of a new day.

4. After fighting with the alarm clock, the person finally drags himself or herself out of bed.

5. As they get out of bed, the mental chatter starts, with so many thoughts in their head about what needs to be done, or what their boss said.

6. They worry about what bills they have to pay, about the family or the partner who did not call the night before.

7. They do not have time to exercise because they slept through the alarm going off.

8. They hurry to shower and during it, they have just enough time to criticize their lives. "Oh no, I look so fat! Why am I so

fat? Why can't I be as slim as that person who gets all the dates?"

9. They rush off to eat breakfast (because they remember it is important to eat). How can they sit down to a healthy meal when there is the fear of being late for work?

10. They grab a snack bar and get dressed while fearing the traffic jam awaiting them on their way to work.

11. Into the car and on the road they go, as predicted there is that ugly traffic.

12. They think, "Oh NO! I knew I should have left earlier, why do I always do this? I am so stupid; my life sucks, and I cannot afford to be late to work again. Why am I still at that job anyway?"

13. By the time they reach their office, they are already pumped full of stress hormones.

The moral of the story is many people wake up stressed, and by the time they get to work, they are super-stressed. Then, it is only a matter of time before the boss, a client or a colleague pisses them off. It is not a matter of "if" that happens; it is a matter of "when" that will happen. Their job stresses them out all day. The end of the day brings its own set of stress as they are once again stuck in traffic wishing they had left work earlier.

14. When they get home, the house needs to be tidied up, and they are in need of some TLC themselves.

15. There many stressors at home to deal with after work that do not allow proper relaxation. The TV, cell calls, text messages, and emails continue to stimulate their nervous system, so there isn't much of the right type of rest.

16. By the time they go to sleep, the body is still pumping out cortisol.

Their body didn't get properly settled into a deep sleep cycle, because of a noisy environment, and far too many stress-hormone cortisol in their system. Does that sound familiar to you? Do some of you relate to that scenario?

Let me tell you that when I tell the above story to my clients and audiences to illustrate how normal stress has become in our lives, and how our health suffers the consequences, they are amazed… but they relate to it. A little stress in short spurts can be well-tolerated by your body. However, living and dwelling constantly in chronic stress mode are not.

Think of a rubber band. Stretch it a bit… no problem. However, no matter how flexible and expandable it is, if you stretch it consistently over time and keep it stretched… it will lose its shape, size, and function, or it snaps!

Stress has its limit in our lives just like the rubber band. Being stressed constantly will cause you to end up with diseases and bad health.

Case study on a Stressful Life

Let us take the life of a typical western woman named Lisa. She's a busy mom with demanding career, a good mom that does a lot for her kids, and a great wife who does a great deal to make her marriage work. Lisa is chronically stressed as she has all these things to do, and she must be 'dead on' all the time. Don't get me wrong … she loves doing them, but has no time to replenish her energy.

She works all week. On the weekends is a soccer mom, looks after her kids, and keeps up with her girlfriends when she has time to take a breath.

Lisa also has her mother and sisters to keep in touch with, as well as her in-laws to please. As you can see, Lisa has many things going on in her busy day, every day. This leads to chronic stress. Remember that rubber band scenario. As the stress continues to mount, Lisa becomes more and more stretched. The chronic nature of her stress starts to become a nuisance to her body because her stress hormones are usually activated.

Let's use the way-back machine here…

I want to take you a few years back into Lisa's life to explain why, at this stage, she is reaching that chronic stress level that leads to stress hormone activation.

Lisa was well-raised by her loving parents, Doug and Mary. Lisa had a great high school education, at the end of which she was forced to pick a career to go into that would give her a good life. She picked engineering, as she believed it was the responsible career to choose. She studied hard because she believed that it would prepare her well for the good life that she was promised. After all, many people had assured her that having a good education and working hard would guarantee success in life for her.

She persisted, studied hard, and attained her degree in engineering. She felt good because she had been taught by society that to live well in this world you need a good job. She did get a job at an engineering firm, and had high expectations that the good life she was promised, would finally begin. She was proud of her achievements.

Working at this firm, she discovered that the job of engineering is no more enjoyable than the study of engineering was. She kept on waiting for that "good life" to begin, and it never did. All that happened was that her enthusiasm was diminishing the longer she worked there. What happened? She became confused because she was working longer hours than she expected, and was dealing with grumpy clients, far more grump than she ever imagined. Life was taking a strange turn away from what she thought it would be for her. She did not realize what the working world would actually bring. Certainly, there was no good life in that job! She also worked for a boss who treated her as if she were a nothing. Her self-esteem dropped to a very low position, and more so as every day went by. She found herself exhausted; she did not give her best at work and lived in fear of being fired.

What to do? Get another job? Sure, but it seemed as if they were all ending up in the same way! What's going on here?

As if this work-related stress and disappointment were not enough, then she is pressured from family and friends to find a man because she's getting, in their opinion, 'older'. They believe that the cause of her unhappiness is her being single. They convince Lisa that being single is a disease, and that she needs a cure – 'get a man in your life, fast' they tell her.

Now she has an added task of finding a man (if only they sold them at the Seven Eleven). Lisa starts putting herself out there to hunt down a man. She uses every trick in the book, gets her heart broken a few times, and her self-esteem plummets even more. As she continues to fail at getting a man to inoculate her against her 'being single disease', she starts to blame herself. She thinks it is because she is fat, ugly, has chubby ankles or a muffin-top stomach. Lisa is developing a dangerous pattern of internal self-loathing that she hides very well from the outside world.

Everyone sees her as a stable woman, but she is secretly going through emotional turmoil. She is convinced that she is a loser as all her friends are in relationships with men. She wonders what is wrong with her. As time goes by, Lisa becomes more desperate in her attempts for dieting and exercising.

The stress in Lisa's life is mounting up slowly. She has stress from a job she does not like, a low self-image, and emotional stress with self-loathing. There is stress from friends and family who are reminding her she is getting older and needs a man. In addition, there is the extra stress that she is putting on herself to lose the weight and to keep up with everyone.

FINALLY, Lisa meets that man who will cure her 'being single disease', and she is very happy. She is in a relationship, but being in the relationship has brought more stress to Lisa. Now she has a new role. She has to be a good girlfriend long enough to get the man to marry her. Her friends and family have increased the pressure because now they expect her to get married to this guy. Lisa has to work twice as hard to maintain that status of the good girlfriend so that he will pop the question, they can get married and live happily ever after.

Fortunately, Lisa and her man do get married; Lisa is happy. They decide to have children. She loves her children and looks after them from Monday to Sunday. She has no time for herself. She now finds that the job of raising the children is falling more on her in an unequal basis. This is not what she and her husband had agreed upon when they were discussing having children. B work and both come home tired. However, she ends up doing more looking after the children than he does.

Her husband believes that he deserves more rest than she does, and that the job of raising kids is her job. You can imagine what kind of arguments go on in that household. Stress prevails when there is turmoil in the house. So when does Lisa unwind?

Some reflection for our own lives and where we are now:

- Did you get any ah-ha moments reading Lisa's story?
- Does this story have any elements that relate to you?
- Have you questioned yourself to find out if where you are in life, is where you want to be?
- Have you ever questioned why you do what you do?
- Have you ever wondered who are you trying so hard to please?
- How often do you take time out to assess yourself and what you truly want?
- Do you feel stuck in a seesaw type of life?
- Who are you really?
- What do you dislike?
- How often do you connect with the inner you for guidance in your life?
- Who has the upper hand in your life?
- Is it your parents, your partner or your nagging friends?
- What do you do daily that brings you peace, love and harmony?
- How often do you take time off and just give it to yourself?

Point Of Reflection

What I have seen as a doctor working in natural health and wellness is that both men and women can relate to this story when I tell it. We all chase dreams that are crushed by superficial pressures from life and other people.   Unfortunately, women have that bonus pressure from our biological clocks, which means marriage and kids, always on the table. Relationships are fun but there is that secret pressure of finding a man and settle down.

For men, it is a choice they can make

For women there comes a time when you are stressed about it, whether you do it yourself or society reminds you of it. Am I right, ladies? Many women live with chronic levels of stress just like Lisa. Statistically speaking, women suffer more chronic diseases than men do. Many chronic diseases are stress-related, and there is a lot of pressure with little relaxation and release along the way.

An example of a chronic disease I often discuss at my events is hypothyroidism, which can be caused by a prolonged, elevated, stress hormone imbalance affecting your metabolism. It is more prevalent in middle-aged women. My opinion is that these women have lived and tolerated low-level chronic stress for years.

These are the women who don't know how to give themselves a break and look after themselves, as they have been taking care of everyone else for so long. They do not have a clue about what to do on their days off, if the kids are not around to look after. They would never think of going to the country to relax, or to the SPA for hot baths, a steam treatment, and a massage. Their pattern of chronic low-level stress has been with them for such a long time that it has become part of them. To them relaxation is party, party, party. That is, unfortunately, far more stressful.

I am a woman – hear me roar

Any chronic stress on the body is never good for you. Having the "I am a mom" excuse does not mean that you have to destroy your health to fulfill that role. I am sure that if you were to ask the children their opinion, they would rather have you healthy, taking care of yourself, and living longer. Many women overexert themselves in their roles as moms, girlfriends, friends, and wives. You are not doing anyone favors by over-working yourself into ill health and un-wellness to be a people pleaser. Instead, deal with the stress, release it, express yourself – and ROAR!

Prescribe for yourself some proper un-stimulated rest. Try a self-aromatherapy session at home, or quiet diners with the TV off. Take extra-long bubble baths with candles around, listen to relaxing soulful music, get a massage with aromatherapy oils, and set the mood with candles. Do yoga at dawn, and make passionate love at sundown.

Go to bed earlier and have that extra hour of sleep, or read a great book in bed with soft music playing in the background to relax you. Have a nice smell of fine incense lingering in your home to relax your senses. For men, who do not like what I am suggesting, find a way to unwind, and relax in an un-stimulatory way that is manly too. When you do, please put your suggestions on my website to help other men. Taking care of yourself is mandatory and so rewarding for your health. Schedule it into your diary agenda; make a date with yourself. Do it for your health. You will feel so much better afterward, and reap all the rewards of a tranquil nervous system that promotes better health and wellness in your life.

Adrenal Fatigue

Chronic stress has its limits. The consequence is the syndrome where your energy is lacking – and this is so prevalent today that it's simply called adrenal fatigue. We live in a world where people are addicted to coffees and energy drinks as their bodies are unable to sustain their own energy levels to function optimally during the day. This is not good!

Your stress hormones are made in two very small glands called adrenal glands. These glands are the size of an almond located above and on either side of your kidneys. They have a limit concerning how much they can continuously produce per day. In time, the adrenal glands will burn out if they have to cope constantly with your super stressful lifestyle.

They will not have enough time to recover between stressful events, if you continuously live under too much stress. They will eventually start producing less and less cortisol hormone because of sheer exhaustion (remember these glands are only the size of two almonds).

When this happens in your body, you can tell by looking in the mirror. You will see dark circles under your eyes, as if you haven't slept for a week, and maybe you haven't. Then, you start to feel easily tired and very low energy levels, especially during the day.

Kind of a drag

Waking up in the morning becomes more of a drag as you do not feel rested. You start to rely on coffees and energy drinks to get you going. You crave energy drinks all day because, physically, you really need them. The classic presentation is a low-grade fatigue that lingers constantly. You will feel a big drop in energy in the afternoons around 2-4 p.m., and you will feel as if you did not sleep the night before.

By the way, the highest sales of energy drinks with caffeine, like Red Bull, are between 2 pm and 4 pm.

The strange thing that happens is that people with adrenal fatigue pick up energy again in the evenings. This occurs because their cortisol, which is supposed to drop, does not drop at all. Instead, it hangs around in their system preventing sleep hormone levels from rising to a normal level. The regular rhythm is that you have cortisol rising during the day to keep your energy levels up and dropping at night to be replaced by your sleep hormone.

Oops – it's backwards

In adrenal fatigue is the opposite. This leads to poor sleep quality and even worse, insomnia. The next day is total exhaustion, with more stimulant energy drinks needed to cope with their daily demands. People think they are addicted to coffee by choice, but I know they are addicted to these stimulants because they have adrenal fatigue, with low cortisol hormone and burnt-out adrenal glands.

Get your cortisol levels checked.

If you are a coffee lover, I advise you to get your cortisol hormone levels checked with a blood test, a urine test, or a saliva test. Start supporting your adrenal glands with some natural herbs such as Rhodiola or Ginseng. Then watch your coffee addiction disappear!

CHAPTER 4

Removing the Extra Baggage

Your Mindset - *Be specific and clear about your success goal:*

Clarity is power.

Confusion is distracting from your goal. Whatever reasons you give yourself for tolerating confusion in your success goals, you need to get rid of them, ASAP. Confusion is just not acceptable when you are looking to be successful in life. It is not a good state of mind to dwell in for long. If confusion arises, then ask yourself the five discovery questions (what, why, where when and how) repeatedly until clarity prevails.

Live clearly in thoughts

To succeed you must choose to live as much as possible in that state of mental clarity. The first thing to be clear about is what your life and identity will be after you have achieved your goal. You have to be clear in your mind what achieving that goal does for you and means to you. Your brain has to have a sharp and clear image of you with that successful life, having achieved that goal.

To lose weight, if that's your goal, then you must be clear on what you are like as a slimmer version of you. You must be able to answer questions like:

- what you look like
- what clothes you wear
- what you walk like
- and where you will live with your new slim body

The more details you can put into your new image, the better. Remember that the brain favors your vision out of all the five senses, so be clear and specific about your success image. Remember that many people have images of what they fear in their minds. They can describe what they don't want with such accuracy that it might scare you as the listener:

- "Well, I don't want another man who can't commit," or
- "I don't want yet another woman who has so many issues and baggage; I am done with those women."

These are all statements you may hear. They paint pictures of exactly what they do not want, and because they say it with such conviction and emotions, it just solidifies the images, and keeps in their cellular memories for a long time.

Would you be surprised, if a year from now, one person calls you and complains to you about the very same problem he mentioned to you yesterday? That person should not keep focusing on what they don't want. Focus draws your attention and concentration and helps recreate that focus in reality. Change the image in your head, and you will change your outcome.

Remove the Unhappiness:

Every time you are unhappy, you create a whole set of thoughts that stick to you and spiral you down, down, down. They make it more difficult to create happy thoughts later when you need them. If you are unhappy often, even if you feel justified to be miserable, and you are just complaining to others about it, you are hurting yourself. Did you know that you are already slowly training your brain to limit your feel-good hormones, your endorphins?

As this unhappiness persists, you start to solidify the neuron connection into the "unhappiness pathway." This pathway starts to ignite and light up faster and faster, making the connection pathways to unhappiness dominate and suppress the pathway to happiness. What you end up with is a miserable attitude that overcomes any happiness you have, quickly and without warning.

Have you noticed how some people get upset over the tiniest things? They explode over minute situations and stay pissed off for longer than others? That's because they have stayed in that unhappiness state for so long that it has become their easy go-to place for responses. What's taken place is that they've rewired their brain neurons to fire in the negative unhappiness pathways with speed and ease. Therefore, that negative and unhappy state of mind you constantly live in, eventually becomes your normal way of being.

Remove Doubt and Disbelief - Paralyzers of success achievement

Doubt and disbelief are the biggest killers of dreams and the biggest promoters of failure. They appear to work on your behalf, looking out for your best interest, when actually they are doing the opposite. Your awareness of this is very important.

Having doubt is truly paralyzing. When people have disbelief – they are frozen in place unable to see clearly. Doubt and disbelief are never on your side and are never your friends. Why not remove those words from your vocabulary? How many successful people do you know that value their doubts? How many do you know that are stuck in their beliefs?

Do you hear successful athletes talk about doubting that they could win in the Olympics? Does doubt empower people to succeed? Does disbelief make people stick to their new healthy lifestyles to ensure weight loss? Think about it carefully.

Doubt and disbelief are deceitful to us, as they appear to be on our side. They both make us act and be "realistic," but this does not benefit us. In fact, doubt and disbelief destroy what little self-confidence and self-power we have left to take necessary actions to lead us to succeed.

Haven't you noticed that once doubt (or disbelief) sets in your mind, it not only kills any excitement and enthusiasm you may have about achieving your success goal; it also leads you to start procrastinating? You wind up with a lot of questions and worries in your head such as:

"I don't know. What if I fail again, just like I did last time?"

The result of having doubt or disbelief, and procrastinating is that you collect enough ammunition to be stuck in a position with no forward movement towards your success goal. Now, you have a bag full of excuses to throw at your success goal every time you think of achieving greatness. Your emotions have already moved from excitement and joy… to fear, pain and sadness.

Don't procrastinate

It's better to decide to not do something, than to sit doubting whether it would be the right thing to do or not, and then procrastinate about it. Doubt pretends to be your friend, but it really is not. Doubt, disbelief, and procrastination, have never led anyone to success in anything in life. It is better to be unrealistic about your success and to go for your success goal anyway, no matter how immense that goal might seem. So, in reality, there is nothing positive or beneficial in procrastination and wallowing in around in doubt and disbelief.

Stop trying to succeed in the realistic sense

If you were to attempt to succeed in the realistic sense, that would surely create you more doubt for you. Success and reality do not really go well together, no matter what anybody tells you, and how hard you say that you are going to try to achieve success using realistic methodology.

The history of successful people shows that one of the first steps toward their successes that they recall includes the elimination of doubt. Many of them started out with an unrealistic approach to society. Consider the example of the billionaire Donald Trump; he was very idealistic about aiming for success while being four billion dollars in debt. Can you imagine what four billion dollars in debt - **$4,000,000,000.00** looks like?

The realistic thing to do when you are faced with a four billion dollars debt is to give up, go bankrupt, run away, and put your head in the sand, in shame and humiliation of the reality of that debt. Trump picked himself up and set new goals and today is one of the richest men on the planet!!

Think about this: Success is not realism.

When success is a decision you have made to achieve, then you cannot follow and submit yourself to the typical "realistic" expectations that society imposes on you. You must put that "realistic concept" aside and make your goals so BIG and apparently unachievable that it scares you, and that might propel you forward. Today Donald Trump has succeeded because of his refusal to doubt himself despite his large debt, and his ability to succeed while overcoming seemingly impossible odds.

No man is an island ...

Another example of a successful billionaire who overcame doubt, and the thought that it was impossible to succeed, is Sir Richard Branson, CEO of Virgin Airlines. He was a struggling artist and was broke. He had an idea to go to an island to try things out. He contacted some real-estate agents, who flew him to an island that he could not afford to buy, but they did not know that. He wined and dined over there as if he was a potential buyer for the island. When the real estate agents realized that Sir Richard was broke and had no money to buy that island, they abandoned him there to find his own way back home. Can you imagine being stranded on an island with no money in your pocket?

Now, the realistic thing for him to do would have been to wallow in self-pity, beg, borrow money, and buy a ticket home. Not Sir Richard Branson! He was unconventional in his expectations to succeed in finding a profitable way home. He turned the situation into an advantage rather than a disadvantage.

He found a way to shuttle planes in and out of the island, and he started making some good money from his venture. He did this very well, even though he was in the middle of what could be perceived as a tragic situation.

This eventually led to the birth of his Virgin Airlines empire, which made him one of the wealthiest billionaires today. Later, he bought the island, and today it's one of the most luxurious holiday resorts in the world. It all started with him being bold enough to fly to an island to buy it, without a shilling to buy it with, but still not giving up on the idea of making things work out on that island for him.

Work on your limitations – it's empowering.

The wonderful thing about working on your own self-imposed limitations is that it gives you the motivation, determination and persistence needed to get you through the tougher times in life. It eliminates all doubts and all disbeliefs as well.

The Firing of Jobs

Another example of an unrealistic successful billionaire person is Steve Jobs, who started a company called Apple that he built from zero and helped it produce some of the most outstanding profits Wall Street has ever seen.

Unfortunately for him, the board of advisors at Apple decided to fire him from his own company. Can you believe that? Can you imagine working so hard to build your company, making it great and the best in their niche, only to be fired and thrown out?

Now the realistic thing to do when you are fired… is to give up, right? Everyone would understand it if you abandon the whole business thing and go do something like take a year off and play hooky. Not Steve Jobs, he was too unrealistic for that. He went out and started another company. He worked even harder on it, and that company did so well that it started to compete with Apple. When the board of directors at Apple heard that Steve's new company was doing great, they called him back in, gave him control, and bought out his new company.

Steve Jobs said he was actually grateful he was fired in the first place, as that lead him to improve himself and to acquire some skills he never would have achieved otherwise. Those new skills made Apple an even better company and made Jobs an even better CEO.

Stories abound…

Many stories exist of successful people who did not follow the realistic route, like Oprah, and Michael Jordan.

The bottom line is that your success goal does not have to be realistic in order to be achievable. It's perfectly acceptable to have unrealistic goals. Those types of goals stretch you as a human being and give you a bigger push.

It is fine to expect to lose weight overnight or to be a millionaire one day in the future while you struggle to pay your bills today. If that is what you truly want, then just to go for it; you will find a way eventually. Being realistic is not always the best way to success. Success can happen to you with unconventional expectations, just as it did to so many before you. Remember, you always have the choice to pick yourself up, dust yourself off, (from a failed attempt) and start all over again. You have the ability to make new decisions every time you have a setback.

Have total clarity about your goal

Be clear and precise regarding your goal. The bigger your success goal is, the better it is for you. Own your success goal! It's yours and a part of you. Just as your arm is part of you, so is your willingness to achieve your goal.

Don't see yourself as different from or separate from your goal, instead incorporate it into your being and your life. Identify yourself with your new success goal regularly by affirming statements such as:

- I am that new slim woman in the making
- I am a rich man in the making
- I am a successful business owner in the making
- I am in the process of slimming down, baby!

You have to become what you want to be, even before it has materialized. You must start seeing yourself having already achieved that success goal, even if others do not see it. Your physiology and the way you carry your body must start changing to reflect that your new success goal is unconsciously supported on your journey. The way you walk, talk, and stand must reflect that of a successful person.

Walk tall, chin up, and suck in that gut. You'll instantly look slimmer when you make those adjustments to your physiology. Looking and feeling thinner in the present moment will speed up your success in the future, while it infuses your goal with newfound energy. Once momentum has set in, then your success goal has no choice but to manifest. Note, however, that you must repeat affirmative statements, and the adjustments to your physiology often enough so that they are engraved into your way of being.

Success is an acquired habit.

You must do some routines that build success, and some may not be much fun to you. You still must keep working at it, no matter how many times you fail.

Persist ...

Just keep going. To persist must become a habit. Ask yourself: "Does a child stop trying to walk because they fell down?" Of course not! Can you imagine a child who is crawling and trying to stand up in order to walk who decides, "I'm not going to walk because I fell on my butt more than once?" That does not happen.

This is the 'child preparing NOT to walk scenario':

- They sit there and give up.
- They say, "I have tried to walk so many times, and it didn't work, so I give up on walking and will crawl for the rest of my life."

Do you seriously think *that* response would ever take place from a normal functioning child who is preparing to walk? Of course not! So, then why do you repeatedly give yourself images of you failing or giving up on your success goal?

Children are totally unrealistic in their attempts to succeed at walking. Yes, when they fall down repeatedly, they just pick themselves up, dust themselves off, and start all over again – no matter what.

As adults, someone taught us that it is more "realistic" to give up on our dreams and our success goals after falling down a couple of times. It's "understandable" to give up if you've "tried hard and given it your best."

Normal efforts mean mediocrity.

There is no one who really wants to achieve greatness, who settles for exerting common (or minimal) efforts towards achieving their goal. To succeed, you have to be prepared to put in so much more than normal or minimalistic efforts.

I believe that by trying to be normal and realistic while pursuing your success goal is the quickest and fastest shortcut to mediocrity. You have to be ready to UN-learn what you learned about success if you want to achieve greatness. Obviously, what you have known, up until now, has not served you to be the best you can be.

What is success?

Success is the indication that you got what you wanted. It is proof that when we say you were born to win – you did just that.

Success takes you out of the norm and demonstrates that you are able to stand on your own two feet. Success is not always a community-shared thing, as it can isolate you overnight from those who do not share the success.

It can be a very lonely place, temporarily, and you have to have to be prepared for that. You must have the ability to be tough enough, no matter how many of your personal group of supporting friends, who hung around when you were stuck and not successful, run away leaving you all alone because now you are. Keep going, build more success. Soon, although you might go through some tough and lonely times, you will survive and emerge a whole lot better off as a human being and as a successful person.

This is why you must not listen to others when they tell you to be "realistic" and aim low, or just do what you know you can do. As popular as this advice might be, if you follow it, then you will simply accomplish sub-standard results, essentially, you'll get what you have always achieved; yes, you will get the same-old results. When you are being "realistic" by the standards of others, you're on the fast-track to mediocrity, and you'll remain in the same old, same-old reality with the same-old views.

If you feel stirred up inside to make a big change in your life and to leap into success, you have to break out of those ideas of being "realistic." By breaking out and making that change, you'll find the way to get through those large obstacles and achieve your success. You must be unconventional; expect obstacles, and be prepared to win anyway, even if it means losing other people's support.

Realistic = ordinary.

Being realistic makes you normal and ordinary. Normal and ordinary people do not succeed; they do not win the Olympic gold medals, nor do they win sport championships. Normal and ordinary people do not end up winning Oscars and Grammys, nor academic achievements. Normal people do not end up changing the world.

Be extraordinary...

There needs to be a dose of extraordinary in life from time to time to achieve success and an extraordinary life. Staying normal and ordinary is just not acceptable, if the fire in your belly is the strong desire pushing you to achieve your success goal. Stop trying to be normal, ordinary and average.

Let me ask you a question to illustrate how being normal is not really the best thing to do. In the dating arena, how many guys show off their "ordinary, average and regular girl" to the public? Not many of them, right?

However, how many guys (and girls) show off and are proud of their "extraordinary person that they've met?" Answer, ALL OF THEM. Everyone secretly craves for the exceptional factor in his or her partners, right? Think about it, and be extraordinary yourself.

Stick to your Plan

Think outside the box. The way you have been thinking, up until now, is exactly what has created the failures you have in your life today. It is a proven fact that your point of view leads you to habitual behaviors in your future. You are where you are because of the thoughts you have been thinking. Change your thoughts by drastically shifting your point of view.

What are you focusing on?

Are you focusing on the potential failure in achieving your goals or do you focus on the success of achieving your goals? Your focus must change to shift your thinking effectively.

You must agree that a millionaire has a different focus in life than a poverty-stricken person. A healthy person has a different focus in life from an unhealthy person. Therefore, you find that different thought patterns exist in people who have different focuses and different points of view.

Some people have success thoughts that arise by success focus and points of views, while others have failure thoughts that arise by a failure focus.

It is never easy to change your thoughts, but it is worth it. It takes repetition and persistence to change your thinking. It is much better to start with a change of focus first, and then change viewpoints. Once you are able to visualize yourself and acknowledge yourself in your new and focused role, rather than changing your thought patterns, success comes easier.

Take Imperfect Actions:

The biggest reason for procrastination is that we have been taught to take only action when things are perfectly in place… and so we are all waiting for everything to fall ideally into place. The longer you wait for the perfect, favorable situation, the more fear and doubt you pick up along the way, and that leads to even more stagnation and procrastination.

The excuse used by most, is that they do not have all their necessities, and therefore, must wait until they do before taking action! This is why most people do not succeed often. We easily forget that our goals do not accomplish themselves miraculously.

How can you win a race if you do not even start it? Often we are paralyzed by fear and don't take action in the first place, and fear is such a powerful soul-gripping emotion. Although many of us have many plans for success in our heads, we usually don't take the action needed for one reason or another.

Many people look for the latest diet craze that works fast. These diets make you take calculated actions that promise excellent results that are never delivered. The diet industry is the perfect example of how people are trained to take action only when they feel it is the norm. An example would be cutting out carbs. We follow what others do, and feel safe to take actions only if others are doing it also.

An example of how this works is the low-carb diet. Just because some skinny obsessed Hollywood person states that low carb is the way to go, and we do it, we tend to punish our bodies with low carbs, even though carbs are the most needed nutrients in the body, much more than the larger amounts of proteins in those diets.

Misery loves company

We take actions easily if we feel others are taking the same risk, "If they are doing it that way, then it must be ok." However, this is often the road to failure, misery, mediocrity and being just average!

There are no set path and actions to success, you just have to follow the success principles and keep on taking imperfect actions until you get there. You cannot rely on what others are doing so that you can do it too. Success does not work that way.

Success is about taking action regardless of what the outcome might be, and knowing that whatever comes up you can keep moving. Do not wait until you know more information on something, or check out who else is doing it before you start taking actions on your success goal... just act! Start somewhere, it does not matter where you start, just start. If your actions do not produce positive results, then you can always dust yourself off, change your direction, and take a new action step in a better way. Just do it! (Like the Nike ad used to say)

Make the move

If you are a young lady, and you want to date a new guy you've met in college, and he is not making his move, then go on and give him a call; don't wait for the perfect time or action plan as it may never happen. Just do it.

If your goal is to be a published author, then start writing that book today; don't wait for the perfect moment.

Start investing, even if it is a small amount; just take those imperfect actions. Perfection will come later. You cannot afford to procrastinate while waiting for the perfect actions to take! You will never be extraordinary if you do not take action.

Take action anyway

The bottom line is, you must take imperfect actions towards your goal. Remember that it is easier to turn a moving car around than to turn a stationary car around. The moving car has something that the other car doesn't… momentum. Momentum is the reason why you have to start taking action and get moving immediately. Momentum is what differentiates the winners from the losers. Once you have momentum then success is inevitable.

You cannot gain momentum without taking actions first. There are no shortcuts, unfortunately. However, it does not matter how you start; it never does. The most determinant part of your success is whether you actually start it or not. If you do not start, that is highly detrimental.

Thinking about building a house and actually starting to build a house are two different things. Many of us have ideas in our heads that we talk ourselves out of and never take action on. If all it took to succeed was to think about something, then we could all be mega successful, right?

It takes action

We cannot succeed if we do not even start planning our action steps, and actually take that first action and then the next one. Do not wait anymore. Once again, just do it!

Be wise

You cannot understand success if you are too busy counting your limitations and your downfalls, or spending too much time wallowing on why things failed, instead of picking yourself up, dusting yourself off, and starting all over again by moving on.

How many of us sit there and overanalyze a break-up situation, over and over again in our minds, instead of just moving on and focusing on what action steps to take to ensure a better relationship next time?

We say men get over breakups faster. Well, no they don't. They just wallow less in the sad part of the subject, and take actions towards getting into something new to replace the loss, i.e. a new woman, a new car, a new group, etc.

Wallowing never breeds success

Men don't wallow, and that's the difference between living with heartache and getting over it! The more you wallow in a negative situation, like a bad relationship, or feeling bad over the breakup, the more negative energy that stays around you keeping you down rather than elevating your vibrations, because you have been liberated. Wallowing around in blame and self-pity does not lead to success. Elevating your vibrations because you are free of a bad relationship does.

SUCCESS AND HEALTH

Success and health are similar; you cannot understand disease in order to get to know health. Success and wealth also go together; you cannot spend all your time understanding poverty to get to know wealth. It does not work that way. What you spend time understanding and focusing on, will be attracted to you on a silver plate. You cannot spend time, energy, and effort understanding chaos and struggles in order to promote peace in life. Have you noticed that countries that go down the path of struggle or war tend to stay that way many years with no clear solutions? When wanting to lose weight, you cannot focus up on the fat in the body and then expect a healthy body to appear miraculously from that focus. It does not work that way. This is why so many people who go on diets with the aim to banish fat from their bodies fail so miserably at it. The focus is on the wrong thing; they get to understand everything there is about the problem of being overweight and focus up on it so much that they bring more of it and keep re-creating it. You cannot focus on abolishing fat if you want a healthy body. There is more to being healthy than just removing fat from your body. The solution is not to waste your time on chasing the weight and trying to lose it. The solution is to start understanding health and to follow the principles of health. Spend more time learning about health, and how to have it in your life. Put effort, energy and money into acquiring more health and wellness skills in your life. Your weight will have no choice but to decrease as your body restores itself to its natural state of health and wellbeing. What you focus upon plays the biggest role on what you achieve in your life. Do you get that overweight and fat people understand more about fat and calories than thin people do? They are really obsessed with the wrong side of the coin.

Support yourself

This sounds strange, but you have to make up your mind that you are going to stand up for your success goal and for yourself. When you decide to chase your success, you will encounter many things and many people against you. It is almost as if problems will be attracted to you even more than usual. With so many things that will go against you, you have to decide from the beginning that you will never be against yourself.

You must be with yourself and for yourself. Your achievement of success will need you to do that. So, learn to stand up for yourself and take responsibility for yourself. You are the only person who can ever stand up for yourself against the world and other people's treatment.

People have a right to have an opinion about you, but what is said to you and done to you personally depends on what you allow and what you tolerate in other people's behavior. What people say and do behind your back, on the other hand, is not your business.

Yes, they are allowed to state an opinion of you, and they will! So do not waste your energy trying to stop people's opinions of you behind your back. Trust me, it was exhausting trying to change what people thought and said about me. Some people will like you, and some will not. It is just life, and you should allow it to happen.

It is better to withdraw from that energy drag

Withdraw from all that and its emotional charge, and rather put your energy into people who love you and think you are amazing just for being yourself.

Your duty is to identify who you truly are as a person and follow your core values. Have a strong foundation on who you are and who you are not. This is what will differentiate you from the opinions of people and will allow you to move forward with success. I suggest to my clients to write down their core values every month, and have them on a small piece of paper in their purse somewhere and refer to it.

A Core Values List is a list of ten qualities that are important to you and your self-identify. You can have on list stuff like:

1) honesty,

2) brave,

3) integrity,

4) loyalty

5) trustworthy

6) friendly

7) truthful

etc...

This helps you remember who you are choosing to be as a person. Remember to look daily at this list once, to remind yourself of who you are becoming.

Learn to Listen

I learned the power of listening when I started my natural health clinic, and increased my consultation time from 15 minutes to 30 minutes in duration. What I quickly discovered was that clients appreciated the extra time much more, even though they paid more for it.

They felt at ease and could open up more about what was going on in their lives. Just this seemed to cure half of the problems that were ailing them. I asked them a few open-ended questions, and allowed them to talk freely about their diseases and problems. It took me a lot of practice, and belief in the power of listening to people.

As you know, we as doctors do only 15-minute consultations normally in medicine, so it is a bit hard to listen to long stories during that short time. The first time that I assisted in a 30-minute consultation was at the natural medical center when I was on a short-term contract to try out holistic medicine.

I sat in consultation for a week with another doctor to get the hang of it. The whole 30 minutes seemed too long to me, and it was strange, to say the least.

I came from the conventional western medicine's approach to treatment, where 15 minutes is all you need to sort out patient's problems during a private clinic consultation. I only knew how to focus on just what symptoms were wrong with patients during that time.

As I sat there on my first day at this holistic medical center, I was stunned to hear the medical doctor talk about what was right with the patient too. I was like "really?" Why would a doctor care about what is going right with a patient? The doctor was talking about what the patient was eating, how well they were sleeping, and get this... even about the consistency of the bowel movements! I thought, "Maybe the doctor knows this patient?" He did not.

This went on from patient after patient, after patient. The whole consultation atmosphere was relaxed and soothing. Being there felt like a pampering session to me; I could not believe working as a doctor could be that much fun and relaxed! It was strange to be at a place of work, and not have the usual work-stresses, tensions, and dislikes that generally go with being at work. (You know exactly what I mean from your own work too, don't you?).

Imagine you go to work at a new company that does exactly what you do at your work, and you walk in there, only to find a strange, relaxed, and laid-back atmosphere that you are not used to! It is the same job as your old one but much more fun, appreciated and relaxed! This is what I am talking about!

As I became more comfortable with the techniques, I could not cope with any other form of consultation. Listening to people became an ingrained habit of mine, and I still have 30-minute health and success coaching sessions with my clients today in my office, online, or via Skype. I just love listening, as it honors people and makes them feel valued.

The secret is in the importance of listening

I quickly learned that many of us don't really know how to listen to each other, truly and honestly. This is true not just in our jobs, in our personal lives as well. We are often waiting for a chance to talk and tell our side of the story after the first person talking finishes speaking, instead of listening. Sometimes we don't even let the other person finish talking before we interrupt with what we have to say about the topic.

To be successful we must learn to listen more and pay more attention to what people say. You have to be able to hear what people are saying to you in a conversation, as what they say might be a clue to your next big break in life.

Make money from listening and solving problems

If you listen carefully to people's problems and pains, then you can put together a solution plan that you can charge money for in the future. Every problem that people speak and complain about is a potential new business venture for you. It is easy to miss people's problems and pains, if you are not listening and are too quick to interrupt with whatever you must say right now, before they have a chance to finish.

Have you heard that saying, "Stop talking while I am interrupting you?" I think it is so true in today's conversations. Think about that one! Do fun experiments for the next day or two, and just observe conversations around you. You'll be amazed of how true this is.

I must admit that I also had to learn how to listen to people. I found it hard at first not to jump into conversations and interrupt them with my ideas and opinions as usual. To clear your mind and actually listen to people is quite a skill. It takes a while for some of us to acquire this skill, if we are naturally chatty Cathy's.

With a little help from my friends...

No man is an island. Your success does not only depend on you; it also depends on the others who are a part of your success team. Learning to listen and paying attention to people will make your success journey much smoother. When you listen, you know who supports you and who does not. You can make better decisions about those around you.

Stay Calm and Focused

In any situation, you always have three choices on how to react. You can react based on:

1.   your experiences

2.   your present situation

3.   your future (how you would like it to be in the future).

Usually, reacting from our experiences is the most common way to react to bad situations. We have preset ideas of what something means to us, and we react automatically when we are triggered.

For example, if something happens at work, like if a less-qualified colleague gets a promotion that you'd been working so hard for. Often we try to transcend the situation and end up blaming ourselves, feeling sorry for ourselves, and feeling anger towards ourselves, instead of spending time analyzing the situation in a logical manner.

What we often find is that the reference point for the excessive reaction is based on previous painful experiences in our past. As we go through experiences in life that we do not deal with adequately, we form opinions and points of views that we store in our brains, which become our future reference points for reactions.

Then, these points of views are called upon to justify and solidify new painful situations that remind us of what happened in the past, even in the slightest way. An example is when you did not get that promotion, your first thoughts might be those of self-destruction such as:

- Here we go again
- I just knew it was too good to be true
- It always works against me
- I am a failure and this just proves it
- Why don't things ever work out for me?

However, the present situation may have nothing to do with the intensity of your past reference point. The reason for things not working out may be something else that has nothing to do with you. If you just stop reacting from your autopilot mode, you may figure out what is truly going on, without the emotional charge. The person that was promoted instead of you may have been the boss's cousin, and his mom interfered in the process.

The point here is that, it is very common to use the past to define the present even when it is wrong to do so. This often enslaves us into the past and does not allow us to move forward into success. This leads us to keep re-creating the same failure patterns, experiences, and behaviors repeatedly in a loop. With such a pattern in our mind, success becomes impossible, and we don't want that.

Frame your new success goal in the here and now

Your new success goal is not based on your past, but in your present moment and the resulting future. In order to achieve your new success goal, you have to learn at some point to get out of your old pattern loop and cut the cords linking you to the past. These cords in your subconscious mind have shaped your patterns and beliefs. You'll only realize their existence when you are in the middle of a challenging situation and find yourself reacting in the same-old way. When the situation is happening, it is hard to change your automatic reactions. Your subconscious is too powerful to be influenced once it has taken over.

Be prepared with a decision – IN ADVANCE

It is better to make a decision before challenging situations arrive to change your reaction, in order to analyze the situation in a calm and relaxed manner. Do not wait for the challenging situation to arise to decide how you are going to react to it. The decision has to be made before the situation arises rather than in the middle of the situation.

Another way – be in the present moment

The second way to handle a new challenge or a situation is to remain focused in the present moment. The ability to remain aware during a situation will determine your success or your failure. If you react to a situation based on your experiences, you dishonor the present moment and go onto autopilot.

Staying present in the present moment is one of the things that most successful people do. They train themselves to do that. When you remain present during a situation, you can make better decisions and find intelligent solutions that are relevant to the problem.

Then, you are able to ask the right questions such as, "Ok, so what do I do here to resolve this? What can I gain from this situation? What direction is this leading me to?" These types of questions keep you grounded in the present moment and will get you the right answers.

It is said that the quality of your life depends on the quality of questions you ask yourself. Being present during situations allows you to ask empowering questions. Have you noticed that there are also some questions such "Why me, why doesn't my life work out, why is it always so damned hard?"

Those questions do not ground you in the present; rather, they take you right back to the past failures and validate themselves once again.

Ask yourself five questions:

In any problem or situation, try using the five basic questions to understand it and keep you in the present moment. I find these questions stop you from resorting to your past reference points in reacting to problems or situations.

Asking questions involve the frontal cortex part of your brain, whose job is to reason it out and find the best solutions. This is the logic part. When you are dealing with solutions to problems, you do not want the emotional part of the brain to fire off first. What you want is the frontal cortex to take over the leadership of the brain.

The fear part of the brain needs to settle down and deal with other things, while the frontal cortex part, the logic part, is dominant. The way you do this is by asking focused questions. Do not give your brain wishy-washy questions, which trigger the limbic system and the amygdala parts of the brain and winds up activating the fight and flight response.

Stick to the format and ask logical questions, and you will get logical solutions. We all actually have the ability to solve our problems with total ease, depending on how we approach it in the first place. If we approach our problems from the point of view that there is always a solution somewhere in our brain, then we will find it.

If, on the other hand, we approach a problem while in an overwhelmed and fearful state, then solutions are going to escape us.

Let me say that again: if, on the other hand, we approach a problem while in an overwhelmed and fearful state, then solutions are going to escape us.

1.   Ask yourself... what exactly is the problem?

Repeat the answer aloud to yourself.

2.   What exactly about that situation do you have a problem with?

Be specific with what the problem is. So many of us generalize, dramatize and exaggerate to make them more difficult than they actually are. You need to learn to stop doing that to your brain. Remember that the human brain sees pictures more than the four other senses. When you bombard yourself with overwhelming thoughts and concepts of struggle to exaggerate your point, you end up forming images of the worst-case scenarios that don't help your nervous system and your stress response.

An example is someone who says they have a problem with his or her job. Well, what is the challenge about that job? Is it:

- The parking space at work?

- The lunchtime?

- The weekly meetings?

- Or is it just the increased workload that keeps you there after hours every single night?

What is the problem exactly and what part of the problem is the core issue? Once you know that, then you can ask what the solution is. What are the actions to take to rectify this problem? Every problem has a solution attached to it. Focus on asking what your solution is. Ask questions and give yourself time to think of solutions. They always come!

3.   WHY?

Why is it a problem for you? What is the real reason behind the one you are giving yourself? Why is it affecting you so much? Why are you afraid of the problem or the situation?

This question, why, is one of the ways to connect to your emotions. You should ask it in a clever way. The wrong question can lead you into a quick spiral of self-pity..

Asking:

- Why is this happening to me?

- Why is he doing this to me?

- Why is life so hard?

- Why doesn't it work out for me?

These types of why questions can lead to fear. Instead of questioning why the problem is happening to you, ask:

- Why is this solution the best?

- Why is this helping or harming me?

You can use this type of questioning to understand better where your focus lies:

- Why am I focusing on problems?
- Why am I not focusing on the solutions?

4. Where?

Where did the problem start? Most often, the solution is near where the problem started. You can also ask:

- Where can I get the solution?
- Where is the solution here?
- Where is this reaction coming from?
- Where is the relevance of this problem?
- Where is this affecting you the most?

These questions help you to pinpoint the exact location of the problem, as well as your solution. It expands your awareness and with that awareness, you have the ability to think up different solutions.

5. When?

The time something started is also important. Many problems do not happen overnight:

- When did this become a problem?
- When did things change?
- When did you start being bothered by this?

Time is always a factor in problems and solutions. The timeframe is important when it comes to achieving your solutions. The awareness of how much time you have to come up with the solution for a problem is also very important. When your spouse is leaving you and walking out the door with her bags packed and is leaving your relationship, may not be the right time to offer stupid solutions.

Time is critical at that time, and instant solutions are needed. If you have six months to do your assignment, then you can afford to take your time! Solutions are time-bound, so act accordingly.

HOW?

Stop yourself from asking yourself HOW questions that can disempower you. Instead, ask HOW questions that will lead you to finding solutions easily:

- How can I resolve this for the better?
- How can I tackle this one?
- How did I get myself entangled in this, so I can un-tangle myself?
- How do I find the best solution here?

This is the last question to ask yourself when you are looking for solutions. By the time you get to this question, you have already asked what, why, where and when questions, so now the HOW is easier. I find it can be harder to start from the question HOW if you do not understand the problem well. However, it is often the first question so many of us ask.

The darker side of how:

It is a tricky question as it can be very disempowering to ask the "how" question first. In some cases, it can empower, but most of the time:

- How did it happen to me?
- How could you? and
- How can I make money when I am so broke?

These questions can be scary and threatening. I tell my clients to ask the how question when the problem is well defined with the other questions first. You want to be empowered so you can succeed.

Power and success go together, so make sure that whatever happens to you, you always retain your power!

Decide to Succeed

The difference between leaders and followers is that leaders make tough decisions with ease when others shy away from decision-making. The ability to make decisions is necessary for success.

You have to be at ease with your ability to make decisions easily, fast and accurately. We all actually have a hidden natural ability to making decisions. We make decisions every single day of our lives. We spend our entire lives deciding. From the time we get up in the morning, we start making decisions. We decide to get up from bed or not to get up at all. We decide to make the bed up or not to make the bed. We decide to brush our teeth, to shower, to eat breakfast, to get into the car, to drive on the traffic to work, or not to bother doing any of those things.

On autopilot

These decisions are unconscious and on autopilot. We are not conscious of the decisions we are making in the mornings, but nonetheless, we are making them. You decided what clothes to wear this morning. That was a decision you made with total ease.

We do things like that every single day. We have been doing it for years! In my opinion, we are all masters at making decisions. We have been making them for all or our lives! We have Ph.D. in decision-making for sure!

The problem comes in when we are faced with a difficult and challenging decision. We tend to shy away, believing the false notion that we cannot make decisions at all. That is not true! That is a poor mindset and a mindset of lacking mental ability. That holds us back. It is not true that we cannot. We make them every single day of our lives.

From little choices to big decisions...

We all have the ability to make big decisions. We may need a bit more time and more information to decide, but we are still able to make that decision.

Here is another fact to ponder:

> *The decision will be made one way or another.*

It will either be made by you or be made for you. So, it is in your best interest to get over that false belief that you cannot make decisions, it is disempowering and will hold you back from your success journey.

Believe in your decision-making skills

Success comes with your skill, and your belief in your decision-making ability. The faster and the more confidently you make them, the more often they will be spot on.

Being successful is acknowledging that you already can make decisions wisely, and you make them with ease every day. Making decisions is a success trait that you need to familiarize yourself with early in the process. Decision-making protects you from harm.

Decide to make decisions

Stop sitting on the fence and start deciding with ease. Get over any silly doubts or fears because… you can do it, as we all can. The other thing about decisions is that they are never as final as you fear them to be. If you discover that your first decision was not the best, you can always make another decision, and another.

The biggest lie in life is that all decisions are final. No, not all of them! Some are, like having a tooth pulled, or having a vasectomy but in cases like that, there are alternatives.

With decisions, you are allowed to change your mind and make a new one that overrules the previous, as often as you want. Your decision to eat an apple today can be overridden by the decision to eat a mango instead. The same applies to your big ones. You can decide to get married to someone today, and then decide he or she is not right for you six months down the line.

Don't wallow in doubt, rather decide, and if you change your mind, decide again. It is ok to make decisions. You are not going to die from making a decision, so just do it!

People who understand success will tell you that making decisions is just part of it. You are allowed to change your decision every ten seconds if you want to. There is no hidden rule out there against it. Fearing to decide is actually a hindrance to you and your success.

No one has ever succeeded by sitting on a fence and not deciding what needs to be done. Success itself is a decision that you must repeatedly make, even when things get tough. You have to keep deciding to succeed even when failure is staring at you in the face. **Even when they tell you to abandon hope.**

When everyone else advises you to give up on your dreams and to get real, you have to decide once again that your success goal is worth pursuing. Making decisions has to become as easy as breathing to you. You cannot have big success goals on one hand, and on the other hand, be struggling with the decision of which healthy ice-cream flavor to go for! Just pick the banana and get on with it.

The way you handle little decisions will form the basis of how you'll tackle big decisions later. Therefore, I suggest you to create a simple system to use with small decisions, as which flavor ice cream to eat, and use that system to help you initiate the logical debate to bigger decisions, such as relationships and marriage.

Have a success MINDSET

One thing that I have understood is that life is so much more than what we can see every day. There is also an invisible world that we don't see. We don't see our minds and emotions, but they are there and affect our daily lives.

I have attended many mindset seminars and have read many books to understand this invisible world, which so much empowers our daily lives. When it comes to success, two mindsets play a role. One is your own mind; you make up and decide to be successful or not. The second mindset is what I call the collective-mindset, where you are subject to the success of the people you spend the most time.

I've heard that your collective-mindset is the average mindset of the five people you spend the most time with. My way of understanding the collective-mindset is through seeing examples of it everywhere.

Rich people tend to hang around other rich people; clever people tend to hang around other clever people; loud and talkative people tend to hand around together as they annoy quiet people. Take a good look around you, and you will quickly notice that people with similar mindsets hang around together! My point here is that you must be aware that when you decide to go after your success goal, you will probably be out of sync with the current people close to you.

Unconsciously, and automatically, you will cause a disturbance for most of them, as you move out of your current collective-mindset into one of success. If the people close to you are not prepared to work on their success goals too, then you will lose them somewhere along in your journey.

You will eventually meet new people to be close to, who will be in the same collective-mindset as your success goal. I am still researching this topic for my next book!

Conscious Mind

There is a lot of data being thrown at us every single minute. Our brains have to sort through so much information coming in from the world and our inner thoughts. Our thoughts ramble on and on, non-stop. Most of the thoughts we have in our heads are just useless conversations.

Your conscious mind is the part of your mind that you are aware of... the one that is non-stop thinking like a chatterbox. It has several points of view about everything that is happening to you.

Your decisions to be successful are made in your conscious mind. The conscious mind can focus your thoughts onto a target of success. This has to be done consciously initially, as there are many useless thoughts in your mind, as all of us have already experienced.

Since the conscious mind is the part of your mind that you have control over, you are able to focus your thoughts deliberately. This does take persistence, but it is possible. A daily focusing routine where you contemplate and think about having achieved your success goals with ease helps you to focus your thoughts.

Even though the conscious mind is only 5% of your total mind power, it has significant input into your success. When you use techniques such as affirmations, visualizations, and concentration to solidify your goals in your mind, you are most likely to succeed. Remember that most people solidify failure or difficulties in their minds, and they achieve that too.

I work with my clients with vision boards, which are visual representations of exactly what they want to achieve. I ask them to have that image so clear in their minds that they can recite it to you in the middle of a deep sleep. You have to see success in your mind first and be connected to it internally, before it can manifest physically.

Affirmations are also another mind technique I do with my clients. You are the person that hears you talk all day. You might as well talk in a way that your mind notices success achievement rather than failures!

Your mindset is what you have set as your level of performance in life. It is yours to change and adjust. No one can really adjust your mindset for you. It has to be done by you and you alone. If you are not sure what your current mindset is concerning success, then I suggest you have a look at the results you are getting in your life.

Results do not lie. They are the reflection of your mindset and the pattern of thoughts, which have been running through your mind. If you want to change your current results, then go to the source of it all, and that is your mindset. Use techniques such as vision boards, affirmations, and repetitions of your success goal.

Subconscious mind

This is the bigger part, the 95% of the mind, and it is not directly under your immediate control. The set of habits you own, and the beliefs that you have stored since the beginning of your life on earth, are stored in your subconscious. Your subconscious mind stores and operates based on a set of beliefs that empower you. Of course, some beliefs are self-limiting, and you must work on overcoming them to succeed.

Many of us are held back because of those stored self-limiting beliefs, and it's where our self-sabotaging begins to occur when we want to achieve a goal. Your subconscious mind has a set point of where your success lies, and it can be hard to shift that set point. You want a smoother success road ahead than working on your self-limiting beliefs, which are buried deep in the subconscious mind. Is it easy to find that easier and smoother road? Nope, but your mind finds it if you work at it, and it will be worth following.

Soul searching time…

You need to sit down, start doing some regular soul-searching and discover what self-limiting beliefs hold you back from being all you want to become. Remember, they are stored in your subconscious mind.

You already have habits and behaviors that should light the way to further clues. Some who want to make more money and who find that nothing works for them, might have a self-limiting belief that money is evil or that making money is really hard work. If you are already working hard at your job, then the idea of working even harder to make money is going to be opposed by your subconscious beliefs. If you are a person who likes people and cares a great deal about what others say, making money will be impossible for you.

Your subconscious self-limiting belief is that rich people are evil. Why would your subconscious allow you to be hated for being rich and evil? It is better to be poor and loved because that is what matters to you.

I strongly suggest you work on your hidden subconscious beliefs; doing this will make your life so much smoother. Your success will be more easily reachable if your beliefs are in alignment with your goal.

There are many seminars on mindset, conscious, and subconscious mind. I did a Mind Power course with Robin Banks and John Kehoe, as I needed to understand the role that mind-power plays in success. I did this initially for myself, then secondly for my clients, so I could assist them more.

Remove the Lack mindset

Lack is more prominent in today's world than abundance. The average person is broke and unhappy. There is more lack every day and everywhere than abundance. And it does not matter where you go, the dominant state of being these days is lack. We lack love; we lack tolerance towards one another; we lack success and, of course, we lack money.

Why is that so? I wondered that question when I was broke. I just could not help thinking that something was not right about the lack in my life. How can we be broke when we work so hard to make money? As I questioned my broke status for a while, I understood that lack starts in the mindset before it materializes in your life. You were broke and lacking mentally way before you became broke financially. Your lack and poverty mindset leads you to create situations where lack of money becomes your norm.

I can tell you that being broke for me wasn't just the lack of money; it also included the lack of clarity, lack of awareness, feeling deeply defeated and powerless in my life. I was incapable of receiving love; I felt the most disconnected from God; I felt like this small person in the corner somewhere, and I could not think about a solution out of being broke.

I just did not believe anything was possible. When I discuss this with my clients, they can relate to it. My point here is that lack of money and being broke does not happen in isolation. There is so much more lack surrounding money that many people who are broke completely miss; they only focus on the lack of money part, and forget the other things that are lurking in their lives, such as lack of creativity, thinking inside a tight box mentality, and feeling limited in resources and help.

I explain to my clients that lack of money and being broke starts first in your mind. I did not know that until one day, I had nothing to eat and no money to buy food. I literally broke down and cried for hours. I was living in a foreign country and going through tough times. I had stopped working as I could not focus on the job, and I lived off my savings, which had run out.

So there I was, broke and miserable. It was only after a couple of hours of crying that I picked myself up off the floor, and started asking questions of:

- How the F did I get to this point?
- How can I be a doctor and be broke?

I started reasoning past my unhappiness and misery to get to the root cause. I was not happy with the "You are here because you have no money" answers. As a logical person, I needed to know what being broke is about. I started to notice that lack was not just in money, but also in many things of my life.

Things had deteriorated so much, and I was not very aware of it. I noticed my thinking had changed; my circle of friends had changed, my body, and my emotions had all deteriorated. There was so much lack in all the five major areas of my life, that money was just the icing on top.

I borrowed some money from friends and family, started to attend self-help seminars, and started re-reading my collections of self-help books. I understood very quickly that my poverty status resulted from my poverty mindset. The road to recovery began slowly but surely.

As I started to work part time again, I made some money and quickly hire my first life coach. Hiring a life coach was one of the best things I have ever done and keep doing in my life. I have had five life coaches so far, and I am looking for my sixth one. I get a new life coach every time I have a success goal to work on. I had a life coach as I was writing this book. On my own, my book took two years just to get started. Having a coach helps your mindset, and that helps you progress easier.

It can be quite hard to work alone on your poverty mindset. It can feel like being stuck in a pothole. Poverty mindset starts slowly, and you won't even be aware of it. The moment you chose to believe in any poverty-based thoughts, either from yourself or from others, you start thinking more and smaller, more limited and more negative thoughts about life. It's like a snowball effect. You begin to attract more and more limiting thoughts. You start to misunderstand life on earth as misery 101 … instead of abundance and happiness 404.

Eventually, this negative thinking will become your habit. At this stage, you're not financially broke so you do not feel the effect of poverty thinking. It is just starting. However, as the habit solidifies in your mind, you even begin to invent thoughts that support your new poverty tone in your poverty-minded thoughts. The repetitive cycle of poverty thinking will fester and feed upon itself. Before you know it, you wake up broke and wondering where did it all go so wrong. Today I teach about the poverty mind-set so that I can share some wisdom, as this topic is common among my coaching clients. Poverty consciousness is a limiting mindset that you inherited from your community to be accepted, to fit in with others, and to be welcomed into the social norm.

Abundance mindset is a far less popular and common state of mind than the poverty mindset. It follows the same but opposite path. Many people are just not aware of the abundance that already exists even in the midst of lack and poverty. We have the ability to go from poverty to riches when we decide to switch from poverty to abundance consciousness. The first step to transcending your poverty and lack state is to find out exactly what your poverty beliefs are. We all have them at some point if we are struggling with lack consciousness.

Some people dwell in the belief that there is never enough money, enough jobs; the economy is crumbling; that money is evil, or rich people are greedy. You have to find out exactly where it is showing up in your life and in your thinking.

It is only through increasing your awareness of your negative, poverty-stricken, thought patterns that you can liberate your mind from repeating these patterns.

From now on, if a poverty-based thought pops into in your head, you must STOP, step back from it for a moment, and confront it by saying, CANCEL, CANCEL, CANCEL – and then rethink that thought from an abundance point of view. You must emotionally separate yourself from those poverty thoughts.

Abundance and prosperity are our natural birthright. You have to be prepared to change your thinking to abundance and prosperity. You are not a human being living in lack. You are always abundant, just like nature and the planet you live on is also plentiful.

The concept of "Lack" only lives in the mind of man (and women), not in your body, not in your spirit, not in your soul, and certainly not in the Creative Force (God), nor the planet itself. The only way that your mind makes you believe in lack or scarcity is to cut off your awareness to your infinite abundance.

Your awareness to your infinite abundance begins with the knowledge of who you are. Let us say that within you is energy, which we have talked about. That energy has the power to create or destroy. Creation is a power, like the power of God that helps you to make life better for yourself, and those you love. You understand that power is driven by thoughts, by images (visions), and by emotions.

Your connection to that infinite abundance is driven by your learning to control your thoughts, your feelings, and the images that you put into your subconscious mind.

Wouldn't you like a lesson in Money?

Money is a symbol, a symbol of success. If you have a million of those symbols, you are a millionaire. If you have a thousand of those symbols, you are a thousandaire. If you have a billion of those symbols… well, you get the point.

And maybe right now you are reading this as a hundredaire, or minus four billionaire – and it doesn't matter. The same rule will apply.

RULE:

What you think – you get.
What you think, see, and feel, you get faster.

Get it?
Did you get it?
Got it? Yet?
Got the message?
GOOD!

STOP THE NEGATIVE, FAILING, SELF-DISAPPROVING WORDS, THOUGHTS, IMAGES, AND EMOTIONS!

How, you might ask me? Not easy. However, there is a way, or two, and we can help you shut down the negations, and pump up the positive – pretty fast. And right now medical sciences have approved one for use in treatment of habits and many disorders, and the other method has been researched and approved for the treatment of stress.

Put them together, you have an ideal method for shutting down the negativism towards life, and opening up concepts and abilities to succeed and prosper. The two methods I am speaking about include meditation and a visualization technique that involves self-talk, or talking to yourself in very positive ways.

Now there are many books written on both subjects, and you can find many good ones, but you do not need in-depth study. What you do need is a method that works.

Let's give you the quick course in positive affirmation writing so you can, consciously and intentionally, put some good beneficial thoughts that open and thrive in your subconscious.

Use the words, I AM at the beginning of every sentence, so that you awaken the power of I AM within yourself. It is an amazing power to be able to say to yourself:

I am a good person
I am a person who thinks right.
I am thinking that I want to be a richer person.
In fact, I am enjoying imagining myself as a richer person.
It feels good to imagine myself realizing the power of I am.
I am now happy, healthy, wealthy, peaceful, joyful, and alive.
Now I am better and better every day.
Every day, I am realizing the power of I am.
Now I am better and better every day.
Every day in every way, I am now better, better, and better.
I am terrific; I am fantastic, and I get what I want.

....

And you have had your quick lesson in affirmative statements – positive affirmations for a better and more prosperous you.

You notice that never once did I say the words, no, don't, can't, won't, should, shouldn't, never in those statements. Those sentences are like dwelling in a world of little smiley faces, all holding hands and singing kumbayah, my lord, kumbayah. Everything is sweet, caring, loving and positive in this world, when a discouraging word is never heard And the sky is not cloudy all day. (courtesy of XXXX Records, Home on the Range)

At the same time, it would be appropriate for you to look at the type of music you are listening to. Does it sound like all things you listen to are good and loving? Is the music supportive of love, prosperity, health, and well-being, or does it represent sadness, loneliness, or stupid behaviors like the earlier example on luck – Born Under A Bad Sign? Another popular one was by the Beatles in the 60s – I'm a Loser. Ask yourself – DO YOU NEED TO HEAR THIS?

Music goes deep into your very soul, and instead of listening to songs that put down yourself, your astrological placement in life, all of society, and shaming good things, you can feel better with songs like:

Can You Feel The Love Tonight, from the Lion King, with Elton John

or

Don't Worry, Be Happy - Bobby McFerrin

Really, the music you listen to affects you. The movies, TV shows, and the news that you watch affect you. Your mind is like the farmer's fertile soil for whatever seed thought is planted, by whatever you think, speak, sing.

Thinking WRONG – "I can't stand it. I can't stomach this relationship." *These are sloppy thoughts, uncaring to your body. You think really bad thoughts sometimes, and you don't do anything about it.*	Thinking RIGHT – I like my life, it's a good life. I love my mate. *Your thoughts are organized, structured and positive, as if you are writing a coaching script for a dialogue of a better future for yourself.*
Speak WRONG – "You dumb sh** you know better." *Whether saying this to yourself, or another – speaking what's on your mind without thinking HURTS. Speaking without thinking of negative consequences, you might even speak negatively all the time.*	Speak RIGHT – "You did better, and can do even better." *You think before you speak and you speak only after you listen to the viewpoints of others. You are considerate, knowing that speaking has consequences. You speak positively all the time.*
Sing WRONG – "Born under a bad sign", "I'm a loser". *Your songs are sad and are stories of a failed life. You sing them from memory because they mean so much to you.*	Sing RIGHT – "I'm singing to the world, you got to let the spirit come in." *Your songs are filled with good and positive energy. They motivate you to succeed in everything you do.*

Everything you see, hear, smell, touch, or taste, affects you. Realistically, you need to have a total transformation in those departments. What is a total transformation? – it's more than a change of heart; it's more than a total makeover; it is a total permanent change in all those areas.

The concept of prosperity and riches

Prosperity, or living in a state of being prosperous, is a mindset, or a state of mind, that everything is riches.

We all have riches in our personal life experiences that have taught us a great deal of what NOT to do be rich. M I can help you a bit with some of them.

The concept of habitual addictions. The truth is habitual wastefulness

Habits – good ones are great. Habitual bad ones – well, you get to judge. Let's just talk story for a moment or two about asinine spending.

Bad habits – alcohol. I can't begin to tell you, as a medical doctor, about ALL the things that fail or begin to fail in the body because people have got this all wrong. Abundance is prosperity, riches, self-created riches.

Abundance is not unlimited alcoholism – and this story will make you laugh, but if you are wasting your money drinking, it should make you cry.

The scene was Corpus Christi (Blood of Christ), Texas. It was a Silva Mind seminar; it was lunch break, and hardly anyone working of developing their minds want to eat lunch, so … one of the attendants, a young doctor, who had studied much of the field of hypnotherapy, and was a studier of the water into wine technique (for use with alcoholics) did a process. Everyone just closed their eyes and listened intently to the instructions; soon they journeyed back in time to the last time they were really inebriated, really, really stoned… and then one laughed… really, really happy and high… three more laughed, totally out of their face blasted… the whole room began laughing hysterically and seemed to be swaying a bit.

Then the instructor said, at the count of three you will be TWICE as intoxicated. Twice as drunk, twice as high, totally spaced out. 1-2-3 and he snapped his fingers and the laughter doubled, and the apparent swaying was more obvious.

Then he said, at the count of five you will realize that you have wasted your fortune on drinking alcohol, using drugs, and you could have been a rich person by now, except for your bad habits. 1-2-3-4-5 snapped his fingers, and the laughter stopped, and the group sobered up very fast indeed. Some people attending spent over $5,000 a year for alcohol. They were sober for a long, long time.

How much money could you have saved had you never spent money on your vices, alcohol, drugs, cigarette smoking, sugary food addiction - sweets like pies, cakes, ice cream, and more? You'd have been a 25-thousand-aire, or a quarter-millionaire or more.

This is a good time to find yourself wondering, "why in the hell did I ever buy this?" (you might think about this, and sing to yourself: "Wasted days and wasted nights.")

Here comes another story:

A friend told me the story of his brother and ex-sister-in-law. It started about how he and his brother come from humble beginnings, and how his brother married into money but found out that his wife had in insatiable spending habit. That was okay while the wife's father was still alive, so he could pay for her Cartier this, and Bonwit Teller that. After a while, her father died, and the woman's ability to pay for this unhealthy spending dried up. However, the house wasn't big enough, so my friend's brother built extra closets, then a bigger house, and as he filed bankruptcy, he realized she was very diseased. He sold all her stuff after she abandoned him, to a second-hand shop where they gave him 10% on the dollar, which he claimed in bankruptcy court. She was long gone.

How many thousands or hundreds of thousands were wasted in that 20-year long marriage? They were millionaires many times over, but it was all wasted by mental disease.

How many thousands of dollars have you wasted? And later, with emotion, tell yourself – aaarrgggghhh! What have I done? The action of wasting money, the emotional toll, will act like a detractor from the flow of prosperity away to you.

When your subconscious gets mixed messages, like: "Every day in every way, I am much wealthier," and then later you think, "I can't afford to buy a good dinner (or whatever) – :

Spend more money foolish stuff, or

Shut off that flow of money.

With either, I suppose, there is the possibility that you might get a lesson (in the area of LOVE, loss or divorce) due to this situation, a lesson you might later regret.

Stop habitual spending

Put the money into a good investment that reaps immediate and accessible funds, but is a long term level of profitability. Stop wasting money. You are leaking out money; those are your symbols of success. That's a bad sign!

Mistake: Not having a good savings program

Risk resistant investments still exist, and some allow you to deposit savings automatically from your other accounts. Granted interest today is not great. Some investments do exist that will allow you a fair interest rate and automatic deposits from other accounts. SAVE – SAVE – SAVE.

Thinking Right about Money

Most people have no idea of what money is. Money is the symbol of your success. When you receive money from your job, it is usually because you do consistently good work, otherwise they would probably get rid of you, or reduce the amount they pay you. So, if you get paid for doing something – you get paid for doing GOOD WORK. Cherish your job, even if you don't love it enough, cherish it, and thank it for what you receive from it, money and benefits and vacation – because without it – you could be living in the streets and looking for food from dumpsters. Love your job, cherish it, appreciate the bosses and sub-bosses, and the paycheck, and the vacation and holiday time. GRATITUDE MEANS A LOT!

When someone does something nice for a child, like buying them an ice cream cone, the child says THANK YOU. That means that the child appreciates the gift, and the thank you remains, and often creates repeat performances from an adult who appreciates the spoken gratitude. So, what does that teach us? Politeness and appreciation go a long way.

GRATITUDE – thankfulness – to an invisible and higher power is the highest form of gratitude, and takes place virtually unspoken, as if in prayer or meditation. Some of the religions today say you must show this prayer at mealtimes.

One thing is clear, there is an energy force in this universe that keeps all things going the way they are. You are a part of that energy force, and have the power within you to make changes, in the way the energy force delivers your symbols of success to you.

Do you want to learn? Then be thankful for this education.

At this point, we are going to move into other areas, and help you adjust some of the attitudes and emotions towards wealth and prosperity, and in the end of this first book, we will give you a daily planner to help you reach your goal.

One goal at a time in the beginning is the path to the greatest success. Now let's get that emotional wisdom flowing.

CHAPTER 5

Emotional wisdom

Emotions are part of our lives.

Emotions make us do many things, some wonderful, some not so wonderful.

How many of us are emotional eaters?

Almost all of us, at some point in time, eat to satisfy an emotional need. Some are chronic emotional eaters, and that is dangerous. Emotions are for guidance only, and they serve us on some level, even the negative emotions qualify as helping us learn.

Often, there is considerable bias against negative emotions, and generally, we try our best to suppress them as soon as they arise. To many of us are still eating and filling ourselves with food, and not necessarily healthy food, to avoid facing some negative emotion over some situation that seems to be going badly.

Forgetting that we learn from the guidance our emotions grant us, we have to handle the situation that the emotion is related to and we – just get stuck. Even if the emotion causes us pain, and even if they are just a form of guidance system, it seems that instead of using the guidance system properly we are just choosing incorrectly and causing ourselves pain. Why? Because we chose to learn from pain. Learning without pain is a better plan.

How do you feel an emotion?

You can do this by attaching a particular meaning to a situation. Then you attach a picture (an emotional one) to it, and also the feeling that you have chosen. So, you have a picture + feeling and that is stored very well in the subconscious for future reference, whether you want it to be stored or not.

Now, there is probably another person in this situation, otherwise, this emotional situation might not exist, or you would be in real trouble if you were fighting with yourself… so for the second person:

You have a picture for them (an emotional one) and the feeling they have chosen. So, you have their picture + feeling, which they've stored very well in the subconscious.

Two points of view

This is why two people can go through the same situation and have two completely different emotional reactions to it. The emotional reactions are different due to the different pictures being triggered in the subconscious memory, by those people involved in the situation. They cannot see the same point of view, because the experience and knowledge based on similar events are from two different lines of life experience.

You cannot expect your partners or your friends to react the same emotional way you do, or you want them to… probably they have no similar point of reference.

In your situation, you are just reactive based on your own stored vault of past feelings and experiences. We all have different lives and don't share life experiences. We are all a product of our own past environment, experiences and meanings.

No two people are exactly alike, not even identical twins have the same emotional reactions to experiences. You must understand this about people and therefore, free yourself from criticizing them for their reaction to any situation you are experiencing. You don't share their background experiences, and so you don't have the right to judge their reactions. Walk a mile in their moccasins here.

Do we want to dump those negative emotions right now?

Anger, jealousy, and envy are part of the negative emotion list we are encouraged not to use. We are taught to ignore negative emotions, to not even acknowledge them. People end up feeling guilty when they have a negative emotion because they are taught not to dwell on it.

Negative emotions are classified as taboo when compared to positive emotions. But are they really? Or are they just a guidance system propelling you to make a change in the direction you are aiming your actions?

Why have negative emotions in the first place?

Why would our perfect and magnificent bodies have negative emotions if it has no use for them? Our physiology is far too perfect and precise to have negative emotions that are meant to be ignored. What if we are wrong ignoring those emotions? What if they serve a bigger role than we realize?

What if they actually serve us more than the positive emotions? What if trying to dampen them with food suppression, or whatever quick fix we can get, is not the answer? What if acknowledging them and simply changing your actions was the answer to negative emotions, instead of running away?

What if they are actually there to strengthen you instead of weakening you? Have you ever wondered what an emotion like anger is telling you? Why would you ever feel angry over any situation or with anyone? There is usually a message behind an emotion like anger? What is that message telling you?

What about the pain of failing?

Pain is a powerful sensation. All of us have attempted and failed miserably at something in our lifetime, and we often feel pain from that... emotional pain.

Perhaps we have experienced some form of rejection; that's a pain of failure and disappointment, along with self-pity and self-doubt.

However, when it comes to weight loss:

Most people have tried several times and have failed miserably. They have probably ended up gaining even more weight than before they felt shame or guilt. Because they feel that you do not just fail at only weight loss, you feel like you are punished for even trying to lose. Nothing is more painful than attempting to do something and ending up with the worst possible outcome.

The feeling of a failed weight loss attempt is a hard thing to handle and come to grips with for most. The added weight gain that they end up with, often causes them to feel traumatized by the whole experience. I have been there. I felt like life was not worth living, and I was the ugliest woman on the planet.

Harder ever day …

Every attempt to lose weight that meets with repeated failure, little by little strips us of our self-worth and self-esteem. It's the path to self-loathing, and we move on that path rapidly as the weight keeps piling on, and still we try harder and harder. We fail repeatedly, and in the end, we hate our bodies.

We end up going for quick and easy fixes as we become more desperate to fix our ever-expanding waistlines. In the meantime, our self-loathing persists and worsens. The average woman hates her body. Our image of the body we have tends to worsen. We always wish we had someone else's body.

When you hate your body, you end up hating your life. Because, whether you want to or not, you must live in that body; your life happens in that body. Life cannot be joyous 100% when you hate your vessel, or vehicle, or space suit for life.

Hating your body begins to make the quality of life deteriorate in other areas as well. You take your body with you in these areas of your life. When you don't feel good about your body, you don't feel good about yourself as a person. Hating something creates negative energy vibrations that drain and exhaust you. You won't have the energy you need to make powerful improvements in other areas of your life.

Needless to say, the marketing of weight loss to the public is amazingly confusing, and certainly doesn't help the self-image of anyone who is overweight. This leads to a worsening of the problem. Many of the dieting or weight loss companies take your self-worth and your self-esteem into account. Thus, if you fail once again, you who will suffer the consequences, not them – they still made profits off you and your suffering, knowing you will return for another attempt at another time.

You must take the responsibility in your own hands, to build and protect your self-worth, self-value and self-esteem. No one can ever really do that for you anyway. Not even the perfect partner in your life, nope!

Only You
Can make the world seem bright
only you can make the darkness light…

Connect to the emotional guidance

At some level, every new goal in your life will evoke an emotional response in you. Some emotions are excitement, happiness, love, or even fear, and worse.

Emotions are your guidance system when it comes to your success goal. How you feel about something is an indication of what and where it is in the process of becoming. Many of us are professional suppressors of our emotional guidance.

Yes, we all have an emotional guidance system that is always accurate, always there for every situation and every new adventure we undertake. While guided by our emotional guidance system, the success outcome for a new goal is always known in advance and felt emotionally before it is undertaken. Just as quickly, as the emotional guidance comes up into our awareness… the suppression and denial mechanism also comes up to try to suppress it and create doubt.

Doubt is the biggest suppressor of our emotional guidance system. An example regarding a new success goal of losing weight… often your emotional guidance system will first lead you to excitement and joy because when you achieve it, it serves you on many levels.

However, what happens quickly is that another state of doubt rears its ugly head and suppresses your excitement, therefore reminding you to be "realistic."

You tend to focus on what your predominant emotions are directing you to fear vs. excitement. A goal that excites you attracts you to it, and a goal that scares you pushes you away from it.

Your emotional guidance system also determines your thought patterns. Your thoughts tend to correlate, to support or disprove, your focus. When your focus is on the fear of the magnitude of the goal… for example, you are broke and your goal is to make a-4 billion dollars in just a few years, that scary goal will bring thoughts of fear and disbelief.

Change your thoughts and…

Many people think they can change their thoughts, but they are not told that this is a vast undertaking, if the focus and emotional guidance do not change first. If fear is your predominant emotion in your focus, then it will be extremely hard to rethink and have a courageous thought. It will be exhausting to keep trying to do whatever you want to do.

Be passionate

Many people have lost touch with their own joy and passion to such an extent that they are not even sure what it means to follow their hearts any longer. I know that I have been there, and I know you have an idea about that. I was so under-motivated, exhausted, and all I wanted to do is sleep, forget about living passionately.

What about your life? What does following your heart mean to you? Which dreams and goals make you passionate? What dream is worth living for to you?

Be Forgiving

Forgiveness is often misunderstood. You do not forgive someone to make him or her stronger and make yourself weaker. You forgive someone else to set yourself free. Once you are free, you are able to achieve your goals with total ease. One of the highest states of being is universal forgiveness. You must understand that life is just as challenging for you as it is for everyone else.

We are all somehow trying to satisfy our needs, in one way or another, and we are all doing the best that we can with the understanding that we have. Everyone has both selfish and noble needs. Sometimes one person's understanding of how well they can best satisfy their needs can infringe on another person's needs.

It is naïve of you to assume that it has never happened to you. This is inevitable. We have all been hurt intentionally or un-intentionally by others. However, blaming others or ourselves over past hurts will interfere with our true ability to pursuit our goals and succeed in life.

Remember that the failure to forgive others or ourselves serves no one, least of all you. Bottom line is you have to forgive to succeed.

Forgiveness is an act of letting the past go, an act of releasing negative energy from your load. When we forgive, we release the pain, the hurt, and the wrongs. When you release the emotional and mental baggage then you are able to release the physical baggage in the form of weight loss too.

Forgiveness helps you lose weight

If your goal is to lose weight successfully, then I suggest you forgive and release hurts from your life. Forgive yourself too and stop judging yourself so damn much. Forgiving is a great act that makes you feel lighter and awesome about yourself. You radiate more energy that is positive to yourself and to others when you forgive and release. We often mistreat our bodies. Forgiving ourselves for mistreating our bodies and ourselves is a great practice.

LOVE more

Anything succeeds with love in it. Loving what you do is a sure way to succeed. It is a creative emotion that always empowers you as a person. What more can I say about this emotion? How many songs in the world are written about this powerful emotion? We have all experienced its amazing powers at some point or another in our lives.

Love is the strongest positive emotion in human history. It plays a big role in the fulfillment of our basic needs, such as the need for security, for self-worth, and the need for significance. It has the most healing and constructive abilities.

We spend our lives seeking it repeatedly. Those who have it succeed most easily. They feel more secure because of it, and are able to take on more challenges knowing that love is there to support them. For so many of us, our sense of self-worth is fed by the fact that we are loved and supported in our quest. After all, if people in our lives love us, then we must be worth loving! The need for significance is one of the biggest emotional forces behind much of our success and other behaviors today.

Our fulfillment in our lives is often driven by our desires to succeed. Most of us want our lives to count for something. Feeling loved by the people in our lives enhances our sense of significance and our self-belief.

 Love is the ultimate positive emotion to lighten your energy and your path towards success and achieving your goal. If you can add love to your journey towards success, that will support your goal.

There are many ways to add love to your success goal.

You can have a supportive loving community of friends and family that cheer you on and support you. You can add love itself to the goal by deciding that 1-5% of your new financial gain will be donated with love to charity or tithing.

You can increase the level of love you have for yourself. You can fall in love with a different part of your body every day, and this will help you with the success goal of losing weight.

You can be creative in putting love in your success goal journey. The Bible says that you should go where you are welcomed … "when you enter a town and are welcomed rejoice, eat what is set before you. Heal the sick who are there and tell them 'the kingdom of God is near you'. But when you enter a town and are not welcomed, go into its streets and say, 'even the dust of your town that sticks to our feets we wipe off against you." - Luke 10: 8-11

Have you noticed how love makes your life smoother, easier, more satisfying, more meaningful, and more enjoyable? Why would you not include it in your success goal? In your everyday life, think of the people you love, who love you and send them loving wishes. It is a good idea to get into the process of radiating love to yourself and to the loving people in your life. I've noticed that the second I feel a bit down, and I project love out into the world to all people, I instantly get uplifted and whatever situation was putting me down becomes easier to deal with and more pleasant.

This will work for me whether I am in a stressful or hard situation, or whether I am confronting a difficult or negative person. Love creates a climate of security in which we can boldly seek paths to our success achievements.

The lack of love in a success goal can frequently lead to difficulty and suffering on the journey to success, or even the failure of the goal. In the context of weight-loss success, it has been scientifically proven now that people who have support during their weight loss journeys succeed more often than people who do it alone.

In the context of relationships or marriage

If we do not feel loved by our spouse, our differences in the relationship or marriage magnify. We view each other in the relationship or marriage as a threat to our happiness and success. We fight for self-worth and significance, and the relationship or marriage becomes a bloody battlefield rather than a paradise!

Release panic

Panic is about seeing the worst-case scenario in your head and fearing it greatly. Learning not to panic is the best lesson I have ever learned throughout my life. I was a master in panic, if they only had degrees! I would panic and freak for hours over big or little situations and get physically sick in my stomach over the tiniest things.

I have an overactive imagination, which has made me panic easily in the past, but today I've learned to stay calm. Fear has no place in your success journey.

I've learned to use the power of my Creator to assist me in many situations, as I know that there is nothing truly bigger than we together are. I immediately ask what is the blessing hidden in the situation? What is the lesson in this horrible situation, which is causing panic? What is good for me in this?"

It was strange how by asking myself these types of questions stopped me immediately from being upset about horrendous situations. I was stopped from the panic attacks I usually had.

It was almost as if those questions commanded a shield of protection on me at that specific moment in time. I actually sat there being grateful for the situation.

Today, I coach my clients to ask questions when they are about to panic as they had before. This question sealed the deal. The question is, "If this situation was actually for my highest and best good, how I would react knowing that it is for my best good?" The answer will pop into your head very quickly. One of my answers was, "I would go on holiday and enjoy the extra time off! I would go see my aunt, and my friends that I haven't seen for a long time; I will look for a job in a city I actually love!"

I am always stunned not only by the questions to ask when great fears arise, but also by the accuracy of the answers in my head that calm down the situation. I was clear and was just fine.

Take charge of your mood

It is harder to be successful when your predominant mood is low and depressed. You may have many reasons to feel depressed, and it is understandable, but it does not serve your purpose to succeed in life. How you feel about yourself and about your life play a role in how much motivation you need to succeed in your goal.

No one can change your bad mood for you

You have to make the decision to change your mood by yourself. Yes, a situation may affect your mood, but the ultimate persistence of the mood is your decision.

If you look at successful people very carefully, you will notice that few of them mope around in low moods. They have control over their moods. It does not mean that they do not go through tough situations that can trigger low moods. It just means that they have learned how to control their moods instead of letting their moods control them. It is perfectly all right to be upset over a situation for a short while, but it is not acceptable to wallow in it and build a house in it!

When you struggle with low moods and lack of motivation, you must do whatever is in your power to change that fast. Have you noticed that once you start with a little low mood and a small depression, you quickly can escalate to full-blown unhappiness and depression if you let it occur? You can end up crying, sobbing uncontrollably, and wondering how you got that far in the first place! Sometimes a good cry is good to release some tension in your being but once again, you cannot stay in that state for eternity, at some point you have to pull yourself out of it. We all do feel low and have a cry from time to time. Do not feel self-conscious if you did it today. I did it a few times.

What I discovered was that once I started feeling bad and low about one situation, it did not take me long to remember other reasons why I should feel bad, even things from my childhood would surface. It was amazing how my memory was triggered by the low moods!

I coach clients that one of the quickest ways to change your mood is to change your body position. Your physiology has the power to shut down your mind activities and take over. Therefore, I suggest you use the power of your physiology if those low mood-causing thoughts flood your mind, and you cannot stop them.

Have you noticed that when you are feeling low, and you get up and go for a walk it seems to clear your head immediately and miraculously, and change the quality of your thoughts? What about listening to a piece of music that you like? Watching a funny movie and laughing to change your state?

Power physiology positions

I make my clients stand or sit in what I call power physiology positions. These positions are basically the ones where you un-cross your body and hold your chin up and look forward ahead. To stand in a power stance: stand with your shoulders down, chest out, chin up, legs apart, arms on your side and looking forward ahead. This powerful position will change your state from feeling sorry for yourself as a victim, into someone who can achieve anything.

Many people do not pay attention to how they hold themselves when standing or whether the message is empowering or dis-empowering. The same thing applies to sitting down, do not drop your shoulders forward and hold yourself closed off, as this sends a message of lack of empowerment. You do not want to slouch on a chair either.

To send a message of power using your physiology will be to do a simple thing of keeping your back straight when you sit. Not only does it state power, it also makes you look taller and leaner. Ladies, this is a sexy move (trust me). You become instantly attractive and interesting to the world versus someone who just sloughs in the sofa.

Learn to incorporate power physiology positions into your daily life to achieve success more easily. It does not cost you a thing to adjust the way you sit on a chair, or the way you stand. It does a lot for your life energy flow and wellness. So why not do it daily?

I insist on it with my clients, and they get good results. If all else fails at least you get to look sexier instantly. Who would not want a bit more sexiness in their lives?

I also advise that you place yourself into a physiology position of power when you have to make decisions in your life. Do not make major decision sitting in a slouched position on the sofa. Stand up tall and make that decision. It just gets you to think differently from that slouched position. You'll have more flowing energy through your being, and you'll feel more alive and with a change in position.

As you practice daily these power positions, you will quickly notice that you feel more alive, more energized, more attractive. You also are more noticed by others, as you are not hiding yourself. It is very motivating to do this daily, as you need all the extra success routines you can do to push you forwards towards your goal.

Make your emotions colorful

Color choice is individual, so I won't dwell on it. The only thing I want to say that colors surround you everywhere and they impact your emotions and your moods. It is a good idea to use color to your advantage.

You have color on your walls, clothes, sometimes lighting, and colored things on your desk, etc.... Some colors energize you and others do not. One of your success routines should include putting more energizing colors around you, or wear them.

Only you know what colors energize you. You need your surroundings and your environment to support you on your path to success, and that involves doing simple things like changing the colors around to provide greater stimulation to you.

CHAPTER 6

A Successful Environment

Your environment is simply defined as that which surrounds you, always. It's what you are living in and, therefore, unconsciously and consciously exposed to regularly. It plays a role on whether you succeed in life. Your environment includes your work - your desk, your work area, your organization of your work area; it includes your car - the condition and appearance of the car you drive; it also includes your home – your dining and your living room, bedrooms, and even your kitchen fridge space.

Your environment includes everything in your life that is in your radar every single day. Your environment and your surroundings have certain energy, and they send a message of their own. Everything that surrounds you is a reflection of where you are on your journey of life. When you go to someone's home for the first time, you can get an idea of them by looking at their environment and the space they live in every day of their lives.

Without them saying a word, you can see if they are close to their family by noticing if they have framed photos all around; you can see if they have a healthy living environment... if they are neat and tidy, or if they are cluttered with things piled up everywhere.

The condition of your daily surroundings sends a message about you to others, and it also impacts you. It doesn't only send a message to the whole world about how neat you are, but also about what you love, what you are passionate about, and your spirituality, etc. It sends a message about you to YOU, the person that sees your environment every single day. You resend the same message to yourself every day in that environment you live in.

If you are looking forward to succeeding in a new goal, then you have to be aware of the power of the environment. You have to adjust some of the thing's around your environment to fit your goal.

The cluttered environment

For example... if there is clutter and dirty things lying around everywhere in your place, you are subjecting yourself to the message of clutter and dirty every day, and it is not a good message. You even make excuses that you justify logically, for keeping your surrounding that way. You may say, "My desk is untidy because I am working on a big project, or I just don't have the time to clean it up; I am too busy right now."

The problem is that even after your finish your big project, your desk remains untidy because now you are used to the clutter, and it has become your norm. Your conscious mind may have a logical explanation for why you live in an untidy disorganized environment. However, your unconscious mind and nervous system will not see the explanation as easily as that.

Your nervous system will store the memory of clutter and associate the situation as something negative, but normal for you. Some people have unconsciously associated clutter to famine and poverty, or with severe relationship breakups and loneliness. Let me ask you; where do you see most clutter and dirt, in rich areas or in poverty-stricken areas? Be careful of the unconscious meaning that clutter has for you. It is better to tidy up than to risk the double meaning of clutter.

Your environment and weight loss

Your personal environment plays a huge role in helping you or hurting you in your goal of losing weight and impacts becoming healthier as well. You have an unconscious image and association of what your kitchen or dining area environment looks like when you are slim and healthy. For example, when you were slim and healthy, your fridge had more fruits, veggies, and healthy juices.

In the kitchen, your pantry and cupboards did not have boxes of unhealthy processed foods in them. Instead, they had healthier grains, beans, and health supplements. Your house was probably neater and tidier because you had more focus and self- confidence. You could invite people over, and this made you clean up a bit more. You probably had exercise DVDs and equipment in your room being used for exercise instead of being used for extra clothes and hanging space. You very likely had healthier snacks such as nuts and fruits at work, and water with you at most times. On your route home, you avoided fast-food joints so that you were not tempted to buy junk food. You probably saw the inside of the gym more often, even if you were there for just a short time. You get my drift. Your environment sent you a message of weight loss and health continuously wherever you were. Whether you were at home, at work, in the car, near your fridge or cupboard, everything reflected health around you.

The same thing can be observed about your success in any other areas of your life. There is always a difference in your environment when you are truly successful, and when you are failing. I strongly suggest that you think back to a time when you considered yourself successful, and note how organized your environment was versus when you're failing at something in your life.

Now back to weight loss example. Have you noticed that when you regained weight, it reflected in your environment? There was less healthy food in your kitchen; your exercise equipment was dusty and often used as a place to dump stuff. Your office had no healthy snacks, and the directions to the nearest fast-food place were on your table and in your car. Your gym membership became just another wasted payment, your cupboard and pantry were full of chips, biscuits, and more processed foods than you could handle.

Your environment sends messages to you all the time. It is one of the first things to clean up and change when you are looking forward to succeeding in life or to become healthier. It is simple enough to do, as you can control it easily. There is an old saying that you are actually a product of your environment, so make sure that it aligns and reflects your new success goal and health target. Please do not ignore this, as you cannot have a negative environment and expect a positive outcome. It is asking too much of your will power to work against your negative environment all the time. Make sure your environment continuously sends an empowering and success message to your unconscious mind and nervous system. It is one of the sure ways that you can effortlessly support your own success goals.

You will have an easier time achieving your success goal or losing the weight and becoming healthy. You cannot have a fridge full of soft drinks and expect you will drink water all the time. This is too much work for your willpower to endure. It will be harder to choose water over juices and soft drinks if they are continuously in your environment. So give all your processed foods away and get some new healthy food that will communicate health to you all day long. This is something you have to do to make your journey into health as smooth as possible.

The one thing I must mention that is always in our environment is television. I have nothing against watching TV, but I strongly suggest that you make a plan and decide how much of it you are going to watch per day, per week, and per month. Please do not leave that up to chance. Watching TV can be a distraction in your environment so be conscious of what you are watching and how much of it you are watching. You will need to make time to work toward your goal daily, and that time has to be scheduled. The same thing applies to computers, cell phones, and radios. You have to take control of the things in your environment and not leave them up to chance only. You have to allocate time for each activity, accordingly and intelligently. In order to succeed you have to do the hard work and be tough on yourself sometimes, and it may mean doing away with useless phone conversations that take up time and cutting out TV programs that waste your brainpower.

Another environmental factor I must mention quickly is self-care. Self-care also forms part of your environment at home: how you look after yourself, your clothes, and even your grooming habits. Take care of your toilets and bathrooms; these are private areas important to you. The things you do for yourself in private are the most personal and reflective of you. Have self-care products in your bathroom that send a message of pampering and looking after yourself. Have beautifying products around you that make you feel good about being you. Taking good care of what you have, and beautifying your body, is very energizing and refreshing. So have those things in your home environment. Anything that you do especially for yourself will motivate you. It will play a role on how you view you. How you view yourself is so important for your success and health. Remember that you are a product of your environment, so clean it up.

Learn from Nature's Success

If you were to define nature as either success or failure, which would you pick? Have a look at the abundance, the beauty, the unity that exists in nature every single day. Is that not successful? We are surrounded by success every single day of our lives on this planet if only we take a moment to acknowledge it. It is always there, working in natural harmony.

It is amazing how success works in our natural environment and all the environment and nature work together, whether we as human beings care about it or not. It is continuously working in harmony, with or without us. A mountain does not stop being a mountain because we do not care about it as human beings; it will be a mountain regardless. The sun does not stop shining because human beings suddenly blame it for skin cancer; it still shines warmly and kindly on us. It has its purpose, which it has been doing for millions of years with or without our approval.

The beauty and tranquility of Mother Nature remind us of the purpose of living. We are not here to destroy things; we are here to part of things. There is already success around us. That energy and vibration are already present. We just need to take the time to stop and "smell the roses," so to speak, and take it all in. We are surrounded by beauty, peace, and tranquility every day and yet most of us live such chaotic lives, full of drama and trauma.

If all else fails in your life, then I suggest you turn and observe Mother Nature for motivation to succeed in your life. Mother Nature already succeeds in what she has to do. The ocean succeeds in being the ocean and providing marine life that feeds itself and feeds the animals and the humans. The sun shines with precision and perfection all over the world. It provides its goodness to the plants for the process of photosynthesis, and ensures that chlorophyll is made for the plants. The animals then feed on the plants to sustain their living on earth. How wonderful is the sun? It energizes all the living and non-living things without any discrimination or segregation. The warmth of the sun is available to everyone and to everything.

Learn from the abundant air

Every single cell of your body needs oxygen in the air for respiration. It is the most life-giving process in your body. It is a vital process. Lack of oxygen will kill you faster than any other forms of lack in the body. The wonderful thing is that air is available everywhere. It fills any container you hold out. It flows into anything and everything. You do not have to earn the right to breathe. You just breathe. It is abundant, and it is effortless.

The success of water abundance

70-75 % of the human body is water; the planet earth looks blue compared to other planets as it is dominated by waters in oceans, rivers, lakes, etc.. Water is the most abundant of all the environmental resources. Almost everything on this planet contains water molecules.

Learn from the abundant land

Have you ever walked barefoot on the sand on the beach and felt a connection to mother earth and just felt energized? Our connection to Mother Nature is very empowering; she nourishes us, sustains us and energizes us. There is an activity called grounding, which is fifteen minutes of walking barefoot or simply sitting with your bare feet touching the ground. You just need fifteen minutes a day to connect to mother earth, and to allow the energy exchange to take place. I suggest you read up on grounding, as it is an interesting and relaxing thing to do regularly.

Learn from the abundant forests

There is no such thing as scarcity in nature and that is just a blessing and abundance. There are seven billion people on this planet and enough resources to sustain all of those people. The trees in the forest play such a crucial role in our health as human that many people take for granted.

Have you noticed that you feel more energized when you are around trees? Have you ever wondered why that is? We breathe in oxygen and breathe out carbon dioxide, while trees and plants take in carbon dioxide that we breathe out, and they exchange it for oxygen that we need to breathe in for survival. This is why you should try to walk in nature where there are many trees to feel energized and more alive, as compared to walking in the middle of an overcrowded polluted urban area. The trees in nature emit oxygen and have a higher oxygen concentration, compared to urban areas where oxygen concentrations are low and mixed with other forms of toxic gases from other places.

Learn from the abundant ocean

Did you know that there are still discovering new species in the ocean that we did not know before? It is amazing that just when we think we know it all, we discover that we do not. It is fascinating how the marine world exists in the ocean that most of us are not even aware. My marine biologist friends have a great time learning and discovering new species in our vast oceans. What a job they have! My point here is to challenge you that what you think about life is only the tip of the iceberg! There is so much more going on in this life of yours you still have to discover, which will expand your mood and show you the success around you every day. We truly do live in a very successful environment, my friends.

Learn from the abundance of rain

Water is amazing. Everything contains water on this planet. From afar, our planet looks like it is covered in only water, as it appears blue in space! Water sustains life and promotes life. You, as a human, are 75% water. Many of us focus on drinking water only when we are physically dehydrated, and that is wrong. You should drink water daily to maintain proper body functions. It promotes health, so would you not drink it? Water has instant healing and transformation capacity. The most available transformational energy is rain. Sit in nature, and you will always feel refreshed and have a better solution to your problems. We get rain easily and freely in most parts of this planet. It brings nourishment for plants and humans in the process. It helps the farmers grow food for us. I personally find rainwater refreshing and cleansing.

I love to watch the rain and think of abundance pouring down on us with so much ease. I cannot help but feel that somehow the rain does bring blessings with it that we should be grateful for, even if it does not affect us directly. However, when it starts to rain, people walk around with umbrellas and get angry when they get wet. Take some time to contemplate and watch the rain drops as they hit the ground from their long travels, and you will notice that those raindrops are the evidence of the transformational energy that heals the earth! Transformational power as it was once vapor that solidified and then liquefied again as raindrops! I suggest you read a geography book about how rain comes about and you will understand the transformational energy I am talking about (it is simply amazing!)

The abundance of raindrops is freely available transformational energy manifesting in our lives, and we do not pay attention. Have you ever noticed how desert places just feel like they are lacking energy? Even on TV, you can pick up the sense that something is lacking when people live in sand dunes where it does not rain! When you look at places where it rains a lot, you notice the healthy plantations and forest. You also feel the presence of good and refreshing energy. This is freely and abundantly available to us if we just pay attention.

My point here is to make you understand that abundance in your life does not have to be a hard thing to notice and be grateful for. If you are struggling to find things to be grateful in your life, then have a good look at the gifts Mother Nature gives you every day. Abundance brings success, and it is all around you every day.

I am not saying to go take your clothes off and get wet in the rain. All I am saying that it is available for you to acknowledge its energy of abundance and transformation into your life. I touch the rain a bit, give a small gratitude acknowledgement of its presence, and I call it God's blessing. One of my old friends complained to me that since he met me, he cannot curse at the rain anymore because I frown on such things. Well, I truly believe in honoring and giving gratitude for the abundance freely available to us, to attract more abundance in our private lives. This is just my personal view of the abundance in nature and my life.

Learn from the abundance of sunlight

Sunlight energy sustains life. Plants need sunlight for photosynthesis, and human beings eat plants and plant products to survive on this planet. Sunrays hitting the skin are an important catalyst process in the production of vitamin D in the body. Vitamin D is an important vitamin that promotes healthy bones and teeth, as well as many other functions, including protecting against some cancers. The body has its own natural ability to make vitamin D if we have enough exposure to the sunlight! Today, unfortunately, Vitamin D deficiency is very common. The lab test for vitamin D levels on the average client is low. Low levels show how little sunlight we are getting these days. It is sad that we are deficient on something that is so abundantly available to us. It is almost like being thirsty when we are surrounded by water, or being hungry when food is all around us. It is a strange phenomenon.

Studies have shown that one hour of sunlight daily improves your levels of vitamin D. One of the most critical roles of vitamin D from the sun has to do with facilitating the absorption and utilization of calcium. Calcium makes up a big part of your body. Your bones and teeth are calcium, and your cells have calcium and sodium channels that assist in the regulation of its functioning. Few people realize that calcium is crucial for our survival. Not just kids and old people need calcium for their bones. Everyone needs calcium for his or her cellular functions. The body will take in just the right amount of calcium from your food. Vitamin D facilitates its metabolism. Our abundant sunlight facilitates Vitamin D production! So many people do not spend any time in the sun at all these days, and if they do, they apply too much sun protection and prevent the absorption of vitamin D into their skin. We work indoors; we drive, and we stay at home most of the times. About 90% of our daily awake time is spent indoors. Sunlight helps to keep you awake during the day as it energizes and de-stresses; it also helps to suppress the production of your sleep hormone, melatonin. This suppression leads us to feel more awake and more vibrant during the day.

Have you noticed that people go to sunny places for holidays? They love to lie on the sun and sun bathe. This brings them such great joy and happiness. This is a clue. Sunlight is a mood lifter. You just feel good with a little sunlight on your skin. Studies have shown that one hour a day of sunlight can produce significant improvement in the mood as well as sleep, in all types of patients and not only those suffering from depression. So how about having your lunch in a sunny area or taking an hour and doing your work on a sunny deck at work? You can move with your computer from your stuffy shady cubicle to a sunny spot. You can start to sit outside after work or before work and experience the sun while you do something. It is just a matter of doing whatever you would have done indoors, outdoors in the sun, and reap the benefits. How about playing soccer or tennis, rather than their indoor versions? How about going for a walk in the sun?

The abundance of the sun and its goodness is available to all. There is so much goodness in the sun for us, and we need to be grateful for that. Abundance and gratitude promote success. I suggest we all pay more attention on what we have in our lives that can elicit an attitude of gratitude.

www.ingramcontent.com/pod-product-compliance
Lightning Source LLC
Chambersburg PA
CBHW060053100426
42742CB00014B/2806